ECONOMIC GROWTH AND
INCOME DISPARITY IN BRIC

Theory and Empirical Evidence

ECONOMIC GROWTH AND INCOME DISPARITY IN BRIC

Theory and Empirical Evidence

Monica Das
Skidmore College, USA

Sandwip Kumar Das
State University of New York, Albany, USA

 **World Scientific**

NEW JERSEY · LONDON · SINGAPORE · BEIJING · SHANGHAI · HONG KONG · TAIPEI · CHENNAI

Published by

World Scientific Publishing Co. Pte. Ltd.

5 Toh Tuck Link, Singapore 596224

USA office: 27 Warren Street, Suite 401-402, Hackensack, NJ 07601

UK office: 57 Shelton Street, Covent Garden, London WC2H 9HE

Library of Congress Cataloging-in-Publication Data

Das, Monica.

Economic growth and income disparity in BRIC : theory and empirical evidence / by Monica Das and Sandwip K. Das.

pages cm

Includes bibliographical references and index.

ISBN 978-9814415910

1. Income distribution--Brazil. 2. Income distribution--Russia (Federation) 3. Income distribution--India. 4. Income distribution--China. 5. Economic development--Brazil. 6. Economic development--Russia (Federation) 7. Economic development--India. 8. Economic development--China. I. Das, Sandwip K. II. Title.

HC59.72.I5.D37 2014

339.2--dc23

2013027371

British Library Cataloguing-in-Publication Data

A catalogue record for this book is available from the British Library.

Copyright © 2014 by World Scientific Publishing Co. Pte. Ltd.

All rights reserved. This book, or parts thereof, may not be reproduced in any form or by any means, electronic or mechanical, including photocopying, recording or any information storage and retrieval system now known or to be invented, without written permission from the Publisher.

For photocopying of material in this volume, please pay a copying fee through the Copyright Clearance Center, Inc., 222 Rosewood Drive, Danvers, MA 01923, USA. In this case permission to photocopy is not required from the publisher.

In-house Editors: Sandhya Venkatesh/Chitralekha Elumalai

Typeset by Stallion Press

Email: enquiries@stallionpress.com

Printed in Singapore

Contents

Preface

This book is about the process of economic growth and its possible linkages with income distribution in Brazil, Russia, India, and China (BRIC). We recognize the fact that the political and economic histories of these four developing countries are completely different. In fact, this diversity in BRIC is our starting point. As we take our journey through this diversity, we trace the economic history of BRIC countries to understand their economic and social institutions. The only common theme in this growth story is the high levels of income disparities and poverty that are observed even during the high growth decades. The connection between economic growth and income inequality is extremely complex and it is necessary to go beyond the simplistic Kuznets curve. To understand the interaction between economic growth, income inequality and poverty, we have developed a theoretical framework that incorporates a mechanism of uniform income transfers in a growth model, where economic growth is the result of accumulation. Income transfer mechanism operates in all countries in the form of a progressive taxation system, pension funds, government's antipoverty programs, employment guarantee schemes, land reforms, etc. One of the conclusions of the model is that it is not necessarily true that such income transfers would invariably reduce growth rates. The relationship between economic growth and income inequality depends on certain initial conditions. For instance, if the initial distribution of income is fairly unequal, growth may induce greater equality. On the other hand, at higher levels of per capita incomes, growth may raise inequality, if the initial level of inequality is not very high. This brings a new dimension in the "inverted-U hypothesis". Based on econometric modeling of growth–inequality nexus, we have looked at the patterns of growth and economic disparities in BRIC countries over long periods of time, including the recent high growth phase. Two inequality measures applied in this study are Gini coefficient and Theil's entropy measures, depending on data availability. Attempts have been made to identify the sources of inequality and the role of initial conditions in determining the patterns of development. Each country's experience is unique, but the theoretical model goes a long way to explain their growth–inequality experience. The econometric work to study income convergence in BRIC is an application of the random coefficient model with samples classified according to different criteria. For instance, using average income as the benchmark, we classify the sample into two groups: the deprived group and the affluent group. The sample classification also provides experiences of low and high inequality subgroups, low and high growth subgroups, and low and high corruption subgroups.

We have benefitted from the comments made in many seminars and conferences where different parts of this book were either formally presented or informally discussed with the participants, such as Eastern Economic Conference and Southern Economic Conference as well as seminars in Jawaharlal Nehru University, New Delhi. We gratefully acknowledge our debt to Manoj Pant and Alokesh Barua of Jawaharlal Nehru University and Prashanta Pattanaik and Aman Ullah of University of California, Riverside. Our special thanks to Michael Sattinger and Michael Jerison of State University of New York, Albany, for their constant encouragement. We are grateful to Skidmore College, New York and State University of New York, Albany, for research grants or seminar grants.

We were able to write significant portions of the book only due to availability of data. We are very grateful to P Bhanumati (Director, Central Statistical Office), Ashish Kumar (Additional Director General, Ministry of Statistics and Programme Implementation), P C Mohanan (Deputy Director General, MOSPI) for all state-level data (beyond what is available online). It would have been almost impossible to include any analysis on Russia without the assistance of JK Galbraith at the Inequality project, University of Texas, Austin. We are very grateful to him for wage data of 88 Russian provinces and Ludmila Krytynskaia for compiling such a large dataset during a summer research project at Princeton.

Finally, we would never have written this book without a "big push" from Rama Das, mother of Monica and wife of Sandwip.

Monica Das
(Skidmore College, NY)

Sandwip K. Das
(University at Albany, NY)

December 2012

About the Authors

 Monica Das was born in 1975 in Dallas, Texas and spent her childhood years in the capital city of New Delhi, India. She received her Masters in Economics from the Delhi School of Economics. In 2000, she was offered the *Chancellor's Distinguished Fellowship Award* by the University of California (Riverside) to pursue a Ph.D. in Economics. In 2006, she was awarded the *International Economic Development Research Annual (IEDRA) Award* by the Export Import Bank (EXIM) of India. Her dissertation was published by the EXIM Bank. Currently, she is Associate Professor of Economics in Skidmore College, a liberal arts college in upstate New York. Her areas of specialization are: Nonparametric Econometrics, Trade, Environment and Development. Monica has publications in professional journals such as *Contemporary Economic Policy, Environment and Development Economics, The BE Journal of Economic Analysis and Policy, Eastern Economic Journal, Review of European Studies*, etc. She contributed to *International Encyclopedia of Social Sciences* and served as consultant for research projects developed in UNCTAD for joint publications in the *International Trade and Commodity Study Series*.

 **Sandwip Kumar Das** was born in 1942 in Calcutta, India. He received Masters in Economics from Calcutta University. In 1972, Sandwip received a *Fulbright Fellowship* to pursue Ph.D. in Economics from the Southern Methodist University in Texas. Upon completion, he returned to India to join the Economics Department of the School of International Studies at the Jawaharlal Nehru University (JNU) in New Delhi, where he spent 30 years as Professor, Chairman, and Dean. Currently, Sandwip is Adjunct Faculty of the Economics Department at State University of New York, Albany, after retiring from JNU in 2005. His fields of specialization are: Trade Theory, Econometrics, Economic Development and Indian Economy. Sandwip held visiting appointments in several Universities such as, University of Iowa (Iowa City), Southern Methodist University (Dallas, Texas), University of British Columbia (Vancouver, Canada), and University of California (Riverside). He edited and contributed chapters to several books and published in journals such as *Journal of Political Economy, Review of Economic Studies, Indian Economic Journal, Indian Economic Review, Economic and Political Weekly, Keio Economic Studies, Journal of Quantitative Economics, Asian Journal of Economic and Social Studies, Journal of Development Studies, Journal of Asian Economics, Journal of Economics and Business, Journal of International Trade and Economic Development, B.E. Journal of Economic Analysis & Policy, Contemporary Economic Policy, Environment and Development Economics, Eastern Economic Journal, Indian Growth and Development Studies, Review of European Studies*, etc.

CHAPTER 1

Introduction: BRIC and the World Economy

The BRIC countries is an expression created by the British economist Jim O'Neill from the Goldman Sachs Investment Bank that stands for Brazil, Russia, India, and China, the four largest emerging countries most analyzed and debated nowadays. These countries have had an expanded level of development opportunities, during the past few years. They have been studied together as they represent a significant change in the global markets after starting the liberalization of their economies during the 1990s. The BRIC countries' gross domestic product (GDP) is responsible for 43% of world's GDP, while Europe and the United States together represent 36%. The emerging countries were also responsible for 70% of the growth of the world's GDP (Arbix and Salerno, 2008). The industrial production in the BRIC countries was very significant during the first few months of 2008, in the beginning of world recession, and they were the ones with the highest rates. China and Brazil had the highest growth rates of industrial production, 16% and 10.1%, respectively. The increase in the industrial production in India (7%) and Russia (6.7%) was lower than that of China and Brazil but still higher than in other important countries as the United States (−0.1%), Japan (1.9%), France (3.2%), and Germany (4.8%) (*The Economist*, 2008). Most observers are of the view that China's progress is disproportionately better than the rest of the members of BRIC and that the emergence of China as an economic superpower is largely responsible for the geopolitical imbalance that has long-term implications. But there is no doubt that the economic transformation that is taking place in BRIC is one of the most interesting developments of the 21st century.

Paul Krugman[1] has argued against grouping these four countries together because they are similar only in achieving high growth rates in recent years and particularly against including Russia whose growth is based on energy resources. There are perhaps a whole host of other arguments supporting Krugman's views. China has a market economy but it is ruled by the Communist Party. Russia was a superpower in the Cold War era and now it has an economy in transition. Brazil's colonial rule ended long time ago, in 1822, followed by a long history of postcolonial rule primarily marked by dictatorship. Brazil's experience in democracy is fairly recent. Both during the colonial and postcolonial periods, Brazil was basically a plantation economy and specialized in the export of primary goods, and its entry into the phase of industrial growth is a relatively recent development. India's colonial rule lasted two centuries, after which it opted for parliamentary democracy. But even during the colonial rule, India had a fairly diversified structure of international trade compared to Brazil. In a postwar bipolar world, India adopted the policy of nonalignment and decided to establish the structure of a mixed economy, with government sector dominating the private commercial sector and economic planning setting the direction for the private sector. This system is popularly known in India as *License Permit Raj* in which the private enterprises are required to get industrial licenses to set up businesses or permits to import foreign goods. It took a long time for India to realize the ineffectiveness of its economic machinery that produced neither a high rate of economic growth nor an equitable distribution of incomes. All four economies are now market-driven but they show tremendous variations in research and development (R&D) efforts, which would determine their future growth paths. Table 1.1 gives some idea of how different these countries are in terms of growth of technology. Russia is ahead of others in terms of R&D researchers per million populations, but China runs the biggest R&D activities in terms of absolute size. In terms of effectiveness of R&D spending in securing patents, the ranking is: Russia, China, India, and Brazil.

Apart from the tremendous impact the BRIC countries have on the world economy, which is expected to become even stronger in future,

---

[1] See Rodrigues (2008).

Table 1.1. Innovation inputs and outputs indicators — BRIC countries (2003, 2004).

Indicator	Brazil	Russia	India	China
Researchers in R&D, 2003	59,838	477,646	117,582	926,252
R&D researchers per million population, 2004	344	3,319	119	708
Spending on R&D ($billion), 2004	5.9	6.8	5.9	27.8
Spending on R&D (% of GDP), 2004	0.98	1.17	0.85	1.44
Scientific and technical journal articles, 2003	8,684	15,782	12,774	29,186
R&D spending ($thousand) per scientific and technical article	682	431	460	953
Scientific and technical journal articles per million population, 2003	47.9	109.1	12.0	22.7
Patents granted by USPTO, 2004	161	173	376	597
R&D spending ($million) per patent granted	376.6	39.3	156	46.6

Note: USPTO: United States Patent and Trademark Office.
Source: Mani (2006).

one would also predict a great deal of economic cooperation among them through trade and capital flows. The former Soviet Union was one of India's major trading partners during the Cold War era, and it was relatively easy for India and Russia to reestablish their old economic ties. Until recently, the amount of legal trade between India and China had not been significant, but things are quite different now and China is a major trading partner of India. Ianchovichina *et al.* (2009) has looked at the long-term effects of the fast-growing economies of China and India on the Russian economy in terms of a global general equilibrium model. The simulation results show that Russia is likely to benefit from terms-of-trade improvements caused by higher energy prices as well as from improvement in the quality and variety of imports of manufactures and services from India and

China. However, Russia may develop the symptom of Dutch disease, with its greater reliance on the energy sector and contraction of manufacturing and services sectors. Subsequent studies, such as Pant (2011), have found tremendous expansion of trade within the group of Brazil, Russia, India, China, and South Africa (BRICS) during 1995–2007, as Table 1.2 indicates. Table 1.2 also shows that China's imports and exports are much more globalized than the other four countries, as its trade shares in BRICS have marginally increased during 1995–2007 compared to others, excluding Russia, whose import shares in BRICS have substantially increased while its export shares show stagnation. India's import shares in BRICS have been uniformly higher than export shares, and import growth rates have been uniformly higher than export growth rates on a global basis as well as within the BRICS group, which is a signal for future balance of payment problems and eventual devaluation of its currency. Pant (2011) has also looked at the direction as well as the composition of intra-BRICS trade. There is ample evidence that Brazil, India, and South Africa have switched to China as main trade partner. For India and Brazil, this has been at the expense of Russia, whereas for South Africa, this has been at the expense of Brazil. Only Russia has diverted exports going to China in favor of India. China has a dominant position in the BRICS trade matrix, followed by India, as India and China account for 80% or more of the imports from and exports to the other BRICS countries. As regard the commodity composition of intra-BRICS trade, it is based on export of low technology natural resources, largely driven by China's demand for inputs. Foreign direct investment (FDI) is the best method of diffusing technology globally. However, the current FDI patterns of BRICS countries have no relation with the trade pattern, which makes one wonder whether intra-BRICS trade would be sustainable in future.

The world recession has impacted BRIC countries in diverse ways and has slowed their growth momentum. Brazil had −0.3% output growth rate in 2009 but recovered in 2010, raising the growth rate to 7.5%. However, low growth rates of less than 3% are projected for 2011–2012 (International Monetary Fund, 2012). The World Development Indicators published by the World Bank show −7.8% GDP growth rate in Russian Federation in 2009 from which the economy recovered in 2010 and achieved a growth rate of 4%, which is much below the growth rate of 10% that was achieved

Table 1.2. Intra- and extra-BRICS trade (US$ millions), 1995–2007.

Country	Flows	1995	2000	2007	Annual growth rates (%) 1995–2000	Annual growth rates (%) 2001–2007
Brazil	Import from World	53734.3	55850.6	120621.0	1.0 (4.3)	13.7 (19.5)
	Intra-BRICS Imports	1035.5	2291.9	17014.4	22.0 (−3.7)	39.7 (42.8)
	Share in BRICS	1.0 (5.1)	4.1 (3.7)	14.1(10.7)		
China	Import from World	132084.0	225094.0	956115.0	1.0 (13.8)	13.7 (30.3)
	Intra-BRICS Imports	6108.7	9782.1	59265.9	22.0 (12.2)	39.7 (51.0)
	Share in BRICS	4.6 (2.6)	4.4 (2.4)	6.2 (5.9)		
India	Import from World	36592.1	52940.3	218645.0	9.7 (7.5)	26.7 (22.9)
	Intra-BRICS Imports	2351.6	4324.9	30746.9	16.5 (4.0)	38.7 (38.0)
	Share in BRICS	6.4 (5.6)	8.2 (4.9)	14.1 (9.9)		
Russia	Import from World	46301.0	33880.1	199726.0	−7.5 (7.1)	34.4 (22.9)
	Intra-BRICS Imports	1372.0ᵃ	2425.0	29541.3	15.3 (12.4)	51.7 (23.6)
	Share in BRICS	2.9 (5.2)	7.2 (6.2)	14.8 (6.5)		
South Africa	Import from World	17436.1	26770.7	79872.6	−0.6 (1.8)	20.0 (16.0)
	Intra-BRICS Imports	952.0	1620.1	12563.4	14.2 (3.9)	40.7 (36.9)
	Share in BRICS	3.5 (3.3)	6.1 (3.6)	15.7 (9.7)		

ᵃExclude South Africa's 1995 import figure.
Source: Pant (2011), using UNCTAD stat database. The figures in parentheses are export growth rates or export shares.

in 2000. From the Reserve Bank of India's data sources, it appears that India had achieved a GDP growth rate in excess of 9% per year during 2006–2008 and the recession in the world economy brought it down to 6.7% in 2009. Though the economy grew at the rate of 8.4% in the following two years, the projected growth rate for 2012 is only 6.9%. Among the four countries, China has exhibited the highest degree of resilience. In recent years, China achieved the highest GDP growth rate of 14.2% in 2007, which declined to 9.2% in 2009 but increased to 10.4% in 2010, as shown by the World Bank's World Development Indicators. However, a report from *Reuters* released in April 2012 indicates that the growth rate in China is weakening, putting the GDP growth rate in the first quarter at 8.1%, which is a downgrade from 8.9% in the previous three months.

What is more important is that cracks seem to have appeared in the internal growth engines of India and China. One important issue that is being widely debated in international and local media is the lack of transparency in governance or simply corruption. Wedeman (2012) claims that the Chinese economy had a chance to enter a dynamic growth phase before corruption reached significant levels. The principal reasons for the recent "intensification" of corruption are the sale of land use rights and privatization of state-owned enterprises (SOEs) or their assets and opaque processes rife with opportunities for looting. Rising corruption financed by the profits from land sales and privatization deals is different from squeezing businesses and getting a part of their profits. The former is akin to reaping windfall profits from the growing flow of value. The total value generated by land sales and privatization is much bigger than the loot captured by greedy officials, who are careful not to hurt the source of profit or growth. By contrast, preying on businesses siphons off value from existing capital stock, thus retarding growth. According to Wedeman (2012), the Chinese Communist Party is continuously fighting against corruption and is trying to achieve a 'stalemate' in its war on corruption. Political, bureaucratic, corporate, and individual corruption in India is a cause of major concern. A 2005 study of *Transparency International* found that more than 55% of Indians had first-hand experience of paying bribes to get a job done in public offices. According to Debroy and Bhandari (2011), an estimated 1.26% of GDP in India is collected by corrupt officials and more than US$ 1 trillion are stashed away in foreign havens. *The Brazil Business* (September 19, 2011) has estimated that in 2010, 2% of the Brazilian GDP disappeared in corruption, and although this is much less than other members in the BRIC club, it is still a substantial challenge for the Brazilian government. Despite some progress, organizing new investment and production remains cumbersome and bureaucratic. It is costly and time-consuming to launch or close a business. On average, it takes more than 119 days to start a company, compared to the world average of 30 days. Stifling labor regulations continue to undermine employment and productivity growth in Brazil. *The Global Integrity Report* of 2010 points out that even though Russian Federation has a solid mechanism in place for the public to request information from the government, freedom of the media remains problematic, which is especially visible in privileged position of the ruling class in the national media. Russia also exhibits a significant implementation gap, meaning that many laws on the books are poorly enforced. Indicators assessing the ability to form political parties, election integrity, and political financing transparency all point to this challenge of implementation. Government conflict-of-interest safeguards and checks and balances are inadequate, with effective oversight of the executive posing a major challenge. Citizen input to the budget process is virtually nonexistent, and there is no legislative committee to provide oversight of public funds. While government procurement has become more regulated and transparent, a professional civil service remains elusive. The national ombudsman and supreme audit institution are relatively effective, although the same cannot be said for law enforcement, which faces routine political interference with its work. Transparency International has been publishing corruption perception index (CPI) for a large number of countries since 1995. CPI is measured in the scale of 0 to 10, 0 being the highest and 10 being the lowest measure of corruption. Table 1.3 has CPI measures for BRIC countries. Among the BRIC countries, Brazil is the least and Russia is the most corrupt country, according to CPI. Brazil, India, and China show a regime change so far as corruption is concerned, while corruption in Russia remains stable.

The theoretical literature (Cartier-Bresson, 2000; Klitgaard, 1990; Mauro, 1997; Rege, 2001; Rose-ackerman, 1999; Tanzi, 1998; Tanzi and Davoodi, 1997; Wei, 1997, 1999) on corruption gives one the impression

Table 1.3.   Corruption perception index.

Year	Brazil	Russia	India	China
1995	2.70	—	2.78	2.16
1996	2.96	2.58	2.43	2.63
1997	3.56	2.27	2.75	2.88
1998	4.0	2.4	2.9	3.5
1999	4.1	2.4	2.9	3.4
2000	3.9	2.1	2.8	3.1
2001	4.0	2.3	2.7	3.5
2002	4.0	2.7	2.7	3.5
2003	3.9	2.7	2.8	3.4
2004	3.9	2.8	2.8	3.4
2005	3.7	2.4	2.9	3.2
2006	3.3	2.5	3.3	3.3
2007	3.5	2.3	3.5	3.5
2008	3.5	2.1	3.4	3.6
2009	3.7	2.2	3.4	3.6
2010	3.7	2.1	3.3	3.5
2011	3.8	2.4	3.1	3.6

Source: CPI, http://www.transparency.org/research/CPI/overview.

that transparency will definitely promote competition and efficiency and thereby promote economic growth. Rose-ackerman (1999) explains how corruption spreads when political, bureaucratic, and economic markets come into contact, creating opportunities for corruption at every level of the hierarchy, from the highest public office to the lowest. According to Cartier-Bresson (2000), corruption in the developed countries arises mainly from flaws in the democratic system; on the other hand, corruption has more devastating consequences in the developing countries, because it has a tremendous impact on the sovereign functions, which is not the case in the developed countries. The greater vulnerability to corruption in developing countries is due to the fact that they are more prone to government as well as market failures. While Klitgaard (1990) extensively deals with personal experience in corruption in Equatorial Guinea, Mauro (1997) identifies the main causes of corruptions as trade restrictions, government subsidies, price controls, multiple exchange rates and foreign exchange allocation schemes, low wages in the civil service relative to wages in the private sector, rent-seeking related to natural resource endowments, and various sociological factors. Rege (2001) has reviewed rules and procedures of government procurement in developing countries at regional, national, and international levels and points out that even in the presence of benefits of joining Agreement on Government Procurement, most developing countries have decided not to join. Even an interim agreement on transparency, cutting costs, with no national obligation would ensure the most competitive prices for goods and services, fair and equitable criteria for award of contracts, and a reduction in the level of corruption. Tanzi (1998) and Tanzi and Davoodi (1997) have discussed the adverse effect of corruption on economic growth, focusing on how corruption distorts the decision-making process related to public investment. They have found evidence that higher corruption is associated with (i) higher but wasteful public investment, (ii) lower government revenues, (iii) lower expenditure on operations and maintenance, (iv) lower quality of public infrastructure, and (v) lower productivity of public investment. These are the five channels through which corruption reduces the rates of economic growth. The studies by Wei (1997, 1999) arrive at similar conclusions. Corruption is a major obstacle to economic development. It reduces domestic private investment, discourages FDI, inflates government spending, and shifts government spending away from education, health, and infrastructure maintenance toward less efficient (more manipulable) public projects.

Though most of the studies cited above deal with the effects of corruption on economic growth and economic development, there are some studies (Bardhan, 1997; Gupta *et al.*, 1998) on the impact of corruption on income inequality and poverty. The study by Gupta *et al.* (1998) is a cross-country regression analysis for 1980–1997 which finds evidence that high and rising corruption increases income inequality and poverty. Specifically, the impact of corruption works through the following channels: lower economic growth, biased tax system favoring the rich and the well-connected, poor targeting of social programs, the use of wealth by the rich to lobby government for favorable policies that perpetuate inequality in asset ownership, lower social spending, unequal access to education, and a higher risk in the investment decisions of the poor.

The concept of a social welfare function is a theoretically complex issue. However, development economics, partly influenced by the contributions of Rawls (1971), makes it quite simple by assuming that social welfare is a function of per capita income, inequality, and poverty, with the effect of per capita income on welfare being positive, while the inequality and poverty having negative effects.[2] Therefore, economic growth is an essential component of development, but it is not enough, as reductions in poverty and inequality are equally important. Development policies revolve around the issues related to poverty and inequality, and many of these policies are redistributive in nature. Many countries, developed and developing, have progressive income and wealth taxes, as well as an income transfer mechanism to transfer income from the above-average to below-average earners to reduce income disparities. For instance, US government has food stamp program for the poor as well as unemployment insurance payments. India and Bangladesh have food-for-work programs for the people below the poverty line. Certain provinces in India have employment guarantee schemes, offering employment for a certain number of days in a year to at least one member of poor families. Brazil provides cash incentives to poor families who send their children to school to control child labor practices. Corruption reduces the size of the intended transfer and diverts a part of it to the politicians and bureaucrats, thereby causing a reverse transfer from the below-average to the above-average earners. As a result, the economy is able to achieve neither a rapid growth rate nor an equitable distribution of income. Greater transparency and monitoring of economic activities of the government by independent entities would certainly reduce corruption. However, transparency is costly in terms of monitoring, establishment of new institutions and government procurement regimes, and training of personnel. The achievement of greater transparency may not even be politically feasible. But there is no doubt that a lack of transparency may dampen the growth process and cause substantial income disparities and poverty. It is also conceivable that in the high growth phase of an economy, poverty and inequality rise mainly due to corruption, creating a misleading impression that

---

[2] See Todaro and Smith (2012), Chapter 5.

there exists a trade-off between economic growth and income inequality or poverty.

Corruption may play an important role in the relationship between economic growth and income inequality. A theoretical model developed in the book is based on the concept of uniform income transfer that redistributes income from the above average to the below average earners in the process of economic growth. We have assumed that the size of the transfer from the above-average to the below-average earner is proportional to the extent of deprivation of the latter, which is not exactly realistic but theoretically convenient. This model takes us far away from the simplistic 'Kuznets curve' and reveals a number of complex relationships in the dynamics of economic growth and income distribution in which initial conditions play a crucial role. One such initial condition may be the level of corruption. In any given period, the relationship between economic growth and income distribution depends upon the initial levels of inequality and poverty. It may also depend on whether the economy is on a high-growth or a low-growth phase. The effect of a change in the intensity of income transfer on the growth process is indeterminate, so is the effect of a higher savings rate or higher return on investment on the growth process. In other words, the growth–inequality relationship is an empirical issue, and theory suggests that initial conditions need to be incorporated in econometric studies through proper sample classifications.

We have extensively dealt with economic, political, and social diversity of the BRIC countries in Chapter 2, starting with their historical background. The excessive income inequality of Brazil has been due to regressive public transfers, less equitable distribution of education, and high wage differentials. Brazil's growth rate is not very high, compared to China, but recent evidence suggests that income distribution in Brazil is improving. Russia is a transition economy, and during the period of transition from a command economy to a market economy, Russia's growth rates have been negative along with high levels of inequality, which is, however, true for all transition economies. Russia's high-growth phase started from 2000, and all available evidence points to the fact that growth has not reduced inequality in Russia and the regional differences in socioeconomic conditions and living standards are very large. However, the latest data on growth and inequality in Russia indicate still high but stable economic disparities. Post-independence growth rates in India, often referred to as 'Hindu rate of growth', were not abysmally low, as it is commonly perceived. But India's high-growth phase started after 1991 when major economic policy reforms were implemented. All available evidence suggests that economic growth has enabled India to reduce poverty but not income inequality. In China, it is fairly straightforward to make a contrast between the Mao Zedong era (1949–1976) and Deng Xiaoping era (1979–1997). The Mao era is characterized by low growth rates, sometimes negative growth rates, but also low income inequalities. However, it is also known for high poverty, particularly in the rural areas. The GDP growth rates during the first part of Deng Xiaoping era (1979–1984) were very low, as China's economy was going through a transition phase. China's growth story began in the mid-1990s. Regional economic disparities were high during the first part of Deng Xiaoping era and these substantially came down during the second part.

CHAPTER 2

Political and Economic History of BRIC

2.1. Brazil

Over the past 30 years Brazil has become South America's most influential country and one of the world's largest democracies, achieving an impressive 7.5% growth rate in 2010, a record high since 1986. The country is rich in natural resources, such as iron ore, and recently discovered offshore oil reserves. Brazil's economy is driven by agriculture, which flourishes in certain regions of the country. The GDP of the Latin America's biggest economy reached 3.67 trillion reais (US$2.21 trillion) in 2010, according to the figures released by the Brazilian Institute of Geography and Statistics (IBGE). To achieve this kind of economic performance, Brazil has gone through a long process of structural changes and economic reforms. In 1900, population was only 17.4 million, which increased to 186.8 million in 2005; the share of urban population went up from 40% in 1940 to 85% in 2006; and the share of agriculture in GDP decreased from 28% in 1947 to 8% in 2005, while the share of industry increased from 20% in 1947 to 37.9% in 2005. Economic growth in Brazil is associated with high income inequality. While per capita GDP was US$3,325 in 2004, Gini coefficient was 0.6 in 2001. Northeast Brazil's per capita income is less than half the national average, while the per capita income of southeast Brazil is 34% higher than the national average.[1]

During the colonial period in the 16th century, Brazil was predominantly an exporter of primary goods. The first major export product was sugar, produced in the humid coastal northeastern region, which turned into a monoculture. Sugar export was profitable for estate owners and

---

[1] Baer (2008). Other data sources used in this study are: IPEADATA (www.ipeadata.gov.brl); Banco do Brasil, *Boletin*, and the IMF World Economic Outlook database.

for those who were engaged in marketing, financing shipping and slave trading, and also for import traders, who imported foreign manufactured goods and foodstuffs. In this export-oriented slave economy, the relationship between investment and income generation was very weak.[2] This sugar economy's only linkage was with the cattle economy in the interior part of Brazil. The sugar export boom began to fade by the 17th century. Agriculture in northeast Brazil remained primitive. The slave system kept human resources underdeveloped and the distribution of income and assets extremely concentrated in the hands of Portuguese and other foreign intermediaries. Profits were spent on imported consumer goods rather than on technical and infrastructural improvements.

A new growth process was launched in 1690s with the discovery of gold in the state of Minas Gerais. Gold production steadily increased between 1690 and 1760, shifting the center of economic activities to Brazil's center-south. The mining sector of Minas Gerais had considerable linkages. The demand for food in the mining center was a stimulus for agricultural production. Rio de Janeiro emerged as a major port. The gold cycle ended in the later part of the 18th century, when most of the mines had become exhausted.

Brazil got independence from colonial rule in 1822. By the fourth decade of the 19th century, Brazil entered the coffee cycle and coffee became the principal export item. During 1821 to 1830, coffee accounted for 19% of total exports and by 1891, this share had risen to 63%. Coffee exports were the engine of economic growth throughout most of the 19th century.[3] According to Furtado (1972), the backwardness of Brazil relative to Europe was due to the privileged position of England as a supplier of manufactured goods and to the lack of a native commercial class, as a result of which the political power was in the hands of the landowners.

The Great Depression had a devastating effect on the Brazilian economy. Export value fell from US$445.9 million in 1929 to US$180.6 million in 1932; the price of coffee in 1931 was one-third the average price in

---

[2] Furtado (1972).
[3] Holloway (1975).

1925–1929. Until 1930s, there were few attempts by the government to plan economic development of the country. The Cooke Mission, which consisted of a group of US technicians jointly sponsored by the Brazilian and the US governments, represented the first systematic and analytical research on the economy. The Mission identified the following factors as obstacle to growth: inadequate transport system, a backward system of distributing fuel, lack of funds for industrial investment, restriction on immigration, inadequate technical training facilities, etc. The Mission recommended the expansion of steel industry, wood and paper industry, textile production facilities for both domestic consumption and export. These policies partly worked but their effects on trade and real incomes in 1940s were rather unstable, as shown in Table 2.1.

In the early 1960s, the Brazilian economy lost its dynamism. Real GDP growth rate, which had reached a peak of 10.3% in 1961, declined to 5.3%, 1.5%, and 2.4% in 1962, 1963, and 1964, respectively. A military regime that overthrew the Goulart government in 1964 started to focus on control of inflation, modernization of capital market and incentives for foreign investment. The period, 1962–1967, was one of economic stagnation, followed by an economic boom during 1968–1973, when the real GDP growth rate averaged 11.3%. The increase in personal income inequality between 1960 and 1970 covered the stagnation and the early part of the boom, as shown in Table 2.2.

Table 2.1. Brazil's import, export, and real GDP, 1944–1950 (yearly percentage growth).

	Export value	Import value	Real GDP
1944–1945	16	6	1
1945–1946	49	50	8
1946–1947	17	80	2
1947–1948	3	−8	7
1948–1949	−8	−1	5
1949–1950	24	−2	6

Source: Comissão Mista Brasil-Estados Unidos para Desenvolvimento Econômica, Relatório Geral, Vol. 1 (Rio de Janeiro, 1954); and Conjuntura Econômica.

Table 2.2. Brazil's income distribution, 1960–1970.

	1960	1970
Lower 40%	11.2	9.0
Next 40%	34.3	27.8
Next 15%	27.0	27.0
Top 5%	27.4	36.0
Total	100	100

Source: Baer (2008), Chapter 5.

The oil shock of 1973 and the National Development Plan, 1975–1979, which adopted an import substitution strategy requiring import of goods supporting the planned industrialization program, raised international indebtedness. Debt service (amortization plus interest), which was 30% of export earnings in 1974, increased to 83% in 1982, forcing the government to adopt the International Monetary Fund (IMF)-supervised program: raising the real exchange rate and reducing domestic demand and expenditure. In 1983, the real GDP growth rate was −3.5%. The period between 1985 and 1994 was marked by inflation and an economic drift and also by a debate between economists belonging to a classical orthodox tradition and neostructuralists. Table 2.3 shows very high inflation rates during 1990–1999.

After 1985, Brazil adopted a constitution that allowed for the expropriation of large land holdings that did not fulfill a social function or were considered unproductive. This allowed many families that were previously homeless or in poor conditions to own farm land and sustain their lives. It also allowed smaller farmers to break the monopoly that large farming corporations had when the land was not shared fairly. The issue of land reform in Brazil is highly controversial due to two reasons. First, it has led to political conflicts as the big landowners have tried to resist the change. Second, land reform may have contributed to regional economic imbalance. The market-led agrarian reform (MLAR) model has been implemented in Brazil through the *Projeto Cédula da Terra* (PCT) since 1998. Landlords have given a warm welcome to the PCT and have preferred

Table 2.3. Annual rates of inflation in Brazil (%).

Year	Inflation rate
1990	2,739
1991	415
1992	991
1993	2,104
1994	2,407
1995	67
1996	11.1
1997	7.91
1998	3.89
1999	11.32

Source: Conjuntura Econômica.

PCT to state-led land reform. Landlords who sold their land under PCT were paid 100% cash. But big landlords as well as owners of productive land did not sell via the PCT process. Only small- and medium-sized farms that were underutilized and abandoned were actually sold. Underutilized and abandoned land comprised 81.6% of all land purchased under PCT. The remainder, the so-called well-utilized land (18.4%) was in fact planted with crops whose market prices have substantially dropped. In short, the so-called well-utilized land is that of bankrupt farms, while the majority of PCT land is in remote, less populated areas, without road access, without irrigation and electrical installations, and far from the local markets. Moreover, the beneficiaries are generally the rural poor, but above the national poverty line.

The beneficiaries are also not the "fittest type", since "they are not experienced in the use of 'modern' agricultural practices and trade". There are reports of manipulation of the beneficiary selection process by local government officials, interested church people, and elite peasant leaders. The internal conflicts within the beneficiary organizations (caused partly by the manipulation by beneficiaries coming from the ranks of the rich peasants and other rural elites) have forced some beneficiaries to abandon the purchased lands (Borras, 2003; Navarro, 1998).

All this puts a question mark on the success of the Brazilian MLAR program.

However, land redistribution has turned out to be extremely important in understanding Brazil's economic performance. Brazil is now the world's largest producer of sugarcane and coffee, and also a large exporter of cocoa, soybeans, orange juice, tobacco, forest products, and other tropical fruits and nuts. It is the world's second largest producer of soybeans. Brazil slaughters 28 million heads of cattle each year. This leads to a production of over 8 million tons of beef per year. Brazil became the world leader in beef exports in 2003 after surpassing Australia. Beef export earns Brazil over $1.5 billion per year. Agriculture accounts for 8% of Brazil's GDP, employing more than 25% of the country's labor force. On a value basis, agricultural production is 60% field crop and 40% livestock. Brazil is a net exporter of agricultural and food products, which account for about 35% of the country's exports (Todaro and Smith, 2012).

The redemocratization process, which began in 1985, resulted in the civilian government assuming the presidency. The former trade union leader, Luiz Inácio Lula da Silva, took the office of the presidency in January 2003. The election manifesto of Lula's party explicitly stated the need to promote rapid economic growth and international competitiveness as a backdrop to achieving social development and equity. The annual growth rates of GDP in 2003–2006 were 1.15%, 5.71%, 2.94%, and 3.7%, respectively. President Lula had two major goals: the pursuit of a macroeconomic policy orthodox enough to impress the international financial community and the achievement of socioeconomic equality sequentially, the former to be followed by the latter. Therefore, in the short run, unemployment stayed high defeating the social objective, though inflation was controlled. Import substitution industrialization (ISI) worsened regional imbalance, particularly between northeast and center-south. Prior to ISI, northeast exported sugar, cotton, and cocoa and imported manufactured goods. ISI led to an establishment of most of the industrial capacity in the center-south. Table 2.4 makes it quite clear.

The regional imbalance was somewhat corrected by resource transfer through fiscal mechanism. The federal tax burden to northeast has been traditionally lower than the country as a whole during the 1960s and the 1970s and intergovernmental transfers to northeast as a percentage

Table 2.4. Regional distribution of GDP in Brazil (%).

	1970	1985	1997	2003
North	2.2	4.3	4.4	5.0
Northeast	12.1	13.8	13.1	13.8
Southeast	65.0	59.4	58.6	55.2
South	17.4	17.1	17.7	18.6
Center-west	3.8	5.4	6.2	7.4
Total	100	100	100	100

Source: Baer (2008), Chapter 11.

of GDP of northeast increased from 0.46% in 1960 to 4.21% in 1974. In the northeast, the federal expenditures, transfer of taxes to state and local governments, and tax incentives minus the tax burden increased from a yearly average of 4.4% of northeastern GDP in the early 1960s to over 6% in the first half of the 1970s. Partly due to the fiscal correction mechanism that was put in place, the impact of the crisis in 1980–1983 was milder in northeast than in the country as a whole. While the Brazilian growth rate during the crisis was −1.4%, northeast grew at the rate of 4.5%, which was the result of the fact that the annual growth rate of investment was −9.7% in the country as a whole and 2.1% in northeast.

Brazil's personal income inequality is very high and persistent over time, and it has deep historic and regional roots. With an income share of the richest 20% of the population equal to 33 times the corresponding share of the poorest 20%, Brazil has one of the highest levels of income inequality in the world. The Gini coefficient for the distribution of household incomes per capita is 0.59. A World Bank Country Study (2004) shows that Brazil's income inequality has probably been overestimated as a result of limitations in the household survey data. Previous analysis also suggests an overestimation of inequality to the extent that cost-of-living differences are not fully reflected. But even with better data, income inequality would still be high. Even though aggregate measures in income inequality do not show much change over time, there have been important income improvements for the poorest, especially since stabilization in 1993, and possibly some further improvements in the past three years. Brazil has achieved major improvements in social indicators, particularly health and education. Although these were not immediately translated into less income inequality, they are likely to improve the inequality situation in future.

According to the World Bank study, the excessive income inequality of Brazil is due to three factors: more regressive public transfers, less equitable distribution of education, and high wage differentials. Many social programs are progressive, but retirement pensions, especially pensions for public sector employees, consume the largest share of social expenditure (above 50%) and are heavily biased in favor of higher income groups. In fact, the share of pensions to the richest 20% in Brazil is more than twice the corresponding share in the United States — 61% versus 26%. Moreover, despite having nearly half the percentage of beneficiaries than the United States, Brazil devotes a much higher share of its resources (5 percentage points above) to these entitlements. The unequal distribution of education in Brazil accounts for 29% of excess inequality. Brazil has a considerable skill gap in the labor force when compared with the United States, Mexico, and Colombia. The percentage of high school graduates — not to mention workers with postsecondary education — is only 35%, compared to 94% and 52% in United States and Mexico, respectively. This reflects a long-standing neglect of and inequity in education that has been addressed only recently through substantial education system improvements. Finally, higher skills premiums (wage differentials by skill level) in Brazil account for 32% of excess inequality. The Brazilian differential has been increasing during the 1990s and is 50% greater than the differential in the United States and also well above Mexico's. This means that the unequal asset distribution is projected into an even more unequal distribution of labor market incomes. Besides, these two factors are mutually dependent. The skill premium — the relative price by skill — is partially determined by the distribution of education (the supply of skills). In fact, this premium has increased over time as a result of both technological change and a relative shortage of highly skilled workers.

2.2. Russia

Even before the collapse of communism, many countries dismantled their authoritarian regimes and liberalized economic systems. Latin American countries did this in the 1980s under the compulsion of the debt crisis. The *troika* of democratization, liberalization, and privatization was on the march even before the end of the Cold War (Kaminski, 1996). Then, what is unique about Russia in transition?

Stalin had built an institution based on the rejection of three Western innovations: market, democracy, and the rule of law. The transition from communism had to be systemic and it had to ideally follow the following steps: a credible constitutional design to set up laws by which rules are to be made; a legal and regulatory infrastructure to assure the enforcement of contracts and security of private property,[4] creation of a wide sphere of economic and social activities beyond the direct reach of the state; and creation of mechanisms and guidelines for an active pursuance of policies designed to contain monopolistic practices and negative externalities.[5] The transformation process involved creating a stable currency and maintaining it by monetary and fiscal policies, liberalization of prices, domestic economic activities and foreign trade, and privatization of state property.

The first democratic government formed at the end of 1991 considered the freeing of prices from administrative controls as a precondition for reforms and a package of legislative acts significantly diminished state control in 1992.[6] However, the operation was not complete. The final stages of deregulation of prices were initiated by President Boris Yeltzin. In 1992, all enterprises were allowed to purchase foreign currencies, either through foreign exchange auctions or directly from other enterprises, but the system of centralized foreign exchange distribution was dismantled. The presidential decree in November 1992 also provided free access for Russian citizens to foreign exchange offices, but it did not deregulate export controls. In July 1992, a uniform market exchange rate of the ruble against foreign currencies was introduced. By 1994, the number of goods subject to export quotas declined. Centralized import was also finally abolished

---

[4] Rausser, GC and SR Johnson (1993), "State–Market–Civil institutions: the case of Eastern Europe and Soviet Republics" in *World Development*, Vol. 21(4), 675–689.
[5] Kaminski (1996).
[6] Dabrowski, M (1993), *The Gaidar Programme: Lessons from Poland and Eastern Europe*, Warsaw: CASE-Center for Social and Economic Research and Friedrich Ebert Stiftung.

in January 1994. Russia had made substantial progress in domestic liberalization after two years of reforms, but its external liberalization process was slow. Multiple exchange rate practices meant additional export taxes, on one hand, and hidden import subsidization on the other. All these had implications for federal government budget balance, which was positive in 1991 and turned into deficits in 1992–1994 (*source*: IMF data). Russia's record in privatization was impressive. In 1993, more than 50% of Russian GDP was produced by the private and privatized sectors.

The socialist system ensured full employment in the state sector. Employees, even with high qualifications, were paid relatively low wages. High payroll taxes were used to finance pay-as-you-go pensions received by all those who worked in the state sector. Socialist countries exhibited relatively low levels of inequality. Transition brought an end to open-ended subsidization of enterprises. The end of "soft budget constraint" meant an end of life-long guaranteed employment. Unemployment appeared, and the elimination of most product subsidies increased the relative prices of essentials, putting a squeeze on the poor. It also meant a disappearance of long queues and a better availability of goods that benefitted those with a higher opportunity cost of time. Russia experienced 38% decline in real GDP in 1993, relative to 1988 — an increase in inequality of income measured by Gini index from 24 in 1987–1988 to 48 in 1993–1995 and greater poverty. The overall wage inequality doubled between 1991 and 1994.[7] The poverty, measured by headcount ratio increased from 2% in 1987–1988 to 50% in 1993–1995.[8]

The consolidation of capitalism in Russia during 1990s was difficult, but the reform initiatives ultimately succeeded in stabilizing prices and restoring economic growth. Cumulative expansion of GDP during 1999–2000 was Russia's best growth performance since 1970s.[9] Table 2.5 shows growth rates of real GDP (%) from the previous years:

But Russian capitalism is far from well functioning. Most enterprises have passed out of full state ownership, but problems of corporate

---

[7] Brainerd (1998).

[8] Milanović, B (1998), *Income Inequality and Poverty during the Transition Planned to Market Economy*, Regional and Sectoral Studies, World Bank Publication, 1998.

[9] Hardt (2003).

Table 2.5. Growth rate of real GDP in Russia, 1991–2000.

1991	1992	1993	1994	1995	1996	1997	1998	1999	2000
−5.0	−14.5	−8.7	−12.6	−4.1	−3.4	0.9	−4.9	5.4	8.3

Source: Hardt (2003).

Table 2.6. Growth rate of real GDP in Russia, 2001–2010.

2001	2002	2003	2004	2005	2006	2007	2008	2009	2010
5.1	4.7	7.3	7.2	6.4	8.2	8.5	5.2	−7.8	4.0

Source: IMF, *World Economic Outlook Database*, April 2011.

governance, the judicial system, and land ownership continue to distort property rights. Market forces determine prices, but administrative controls keep key tariffs for energy, transport, and communal services well below market levels. Unaddressed consequences of the August 1998 financial collapse continue to plague banking system and foreign capital inflow. During 1990–2000, income inequality had a steady and rising trend. Galbraith *et al.* (2004) points out that both interregional and sectoral inequality, measured by the Theil entropy index, show rising trend.

Income inequality has almost doubled since the end of the Communist era. Inequality has increased sharply during the years of transition, followed by a moderate decline during the late 1990s and early 2000s because of the 1998 financial crash that briefly narrowed the gap between the rich and the poor. After that, inequality has grown slowly and steadily. As of 2008, Gini index is 42.3. Russia's growth performance after 2000 has been quite impressive, as indicated by Table 2.6, which shows yearly growth rates of real GDP.

The prolonged boom of 2000s has increased incomes across the board, but boosted incomes at the top faster than those at the bottom. Thus, a fast-growing Russian economy did not reverse the rising inequality trends of the previous decade. A study by Remington (2011) has shown that both aggregate interpersonal inequality, measured by

Gini coefficient, and interregional inequality had a rising trend during 1992–2009. Decentralization, commercialization, and privatization of public services have reinforced economic disparities in labor market, where skill is rewarded and women's wages lose ground to men's wages.

Wage-setting procedures in the Russian public sector are obsolete and have hardly changed since the Socialist era. In market economies, public sector wages are set either through collective bargaining or through special monitoring procedures. The aim of both procedures is to tie public sector wages to the wages of "comparable" private sector workers. In Russia, wage-setting in the public sector is largely a politically driven exercise — the parliament adopts the minimum wage level and the government sets a progression scale. In real life, wages in the Russian public sector depend on generosity of local budgets, specific positions of heads of budget organizations in local elites, and access to non-budget funds. This leads to substantial underpay of many workers in this sector and to high variation of wages within the public sector. Pay reform in the public sector should not come to mere wage increase (exactly what is currently done — private sector wages rapidly restore the gap). It should involve certain deregulation of labor protection legislation to allow employment reductions in the public sector and measures to increase the efficiency of public services provision. Lukyanova (2006) has done a study on wage inequality in Russia, separated from the overall income inequality. If the problem of wage inequality is studied in the context of income inequality, policy recommendations are usually confined to the suggestions to compensate for income disparities that emerge from market sources (wages, profits, and rents) by social transfers. In other words, policy recommendations imply income redistribution that leads to efficiency losses and distortion of work incentives. Putting the problem of wage inequality in the context of labor markets will allow designing less distorting tools of income policy.

Lukyanova (2006) shows that wage inequality, measured by Gini index, has increased in all transition economies (CEE, Baltic, and CIS countries) during 1989–2002, and it seems that the growth rate of wage inequality in Russia has been the highest among these economies during this period. The study also shows that wage inequality in Russia is not a temporary phenomenon. Differences in individual earnings are persistent — they are not smoothed over the life cycle, returns to experience are negligibly low.

Persistence of high pay differentials has important policy implications. High wage inequality and existence of the low pay trap may lead to political instability, growth of informal economy, emergence of underclass and lower long-run rates of economic growth as a result of underinvestment into human capital. Since low pay is a not transitory experience in the beginning of working career, measures aimed at reducing labor market poverty should be brought to the top policy agenda.

The major conclusions of this study are as follows. In Russia, interindustry wage differentials are the most significant contributor to wage differentiation with the lowest (conditional) wages in agriculture and budget-funded industries. Low-paid workers tend to be employed in the sectors that are traditionally closed from competition. Therefore, remedies should be twofold: introduction of more competition and pay reform in the budget sector. Decomposition of wage inequality indicates that — other things being equal — demographic variables (mainly gender and region) explain large proportion of wage dispersion (over 40% of the explained variation and 15% of total variation). These findings suggest that there might be some scope for policies targeted on these attributes. Previous research has shown that gender wage gap can be mainly attributed to high professional and occupational segregation. This warrants special measures that would ensure equal opportunities for men and women at the labor market, equal access to jobs in the private sector, and equal rights for promotion. Regional pay differentials require measures aimed at leveling living conditions and lowering migration barriers. Housing reform and enhancing availability of mortgages are the key steps of such policy.

The World Bank study (2005) has looked at poverty and development policy in Russian Federation during 1997–2002, as well as the growth-poverty linkages through the labor market. The study also deals with the contribution of growth and inequality to the recent poverty reduction. It also explores the expected impact of Russia's accession to World Trade Organization (WTO) on overall growth and poverty.

Following the 1998 financial crisis, a steep drop in consumption occurred across all income groups. This drop was even greater for the poor. In 1999, due to the collapse in incomes and jump in inequality, poverty levels reached an all-time high for the transition period. Of every 10 people, 4 people slipped into poverty, not being able to meet nutritional and other basic needs. Luckily, economic rebound after the crisis was both impressive and broad-based, though uneven both in its sectoral and regional distribution. This increased the demand for labor and led to wage hikes, higher employment and extended working hours. In addition to higher earnings, households benefited from the higher oil revenues earned by the government, which was able to substantially reduce arrears in wages and social benefits and raise pensions and public sector wages, as well as public expenditure on social policies, which was drastically cut in real term in the aftermath of the 1998 crisis. Although the recovery period was accompanied by an increase in consumption for everyone, the increase was greatest for the poorest groups, making the 1999–2002 growth pro-poor. Russia succeeded in cutting poverty (headcount ratio) in half, between 1999 and 2002, from 41.5% in 1999 to 19.6% in 2002.

The World Bank study also shows that the regional differences in socioeconomic conditions and living standards are very large in Russia. Gross regional product (GRP) per capita in the richest region is 67 times that of the poorest region in nominal terms and 33 times in real terms, when regional price differences are accounted for. Real consumption per capita in 2002 in the richest region was three times that in the poorest region. The poorest regions include some regions in the North Caucasus, South Siberia, and Central Russia. The richest regions include resource-rich regions in Siberia, the Far East, and the European North, and also Moscow City. However, the regions did not diverge with the after-crisis recovery, which was broad-based and benefited both rich and poor regions. Inequality among the regions remained stable in the 1997–2002 periods and declined somewhat. The study has done a decomposition of overall inequality in consumption into two components: interregional inequality and intraregional inequality. Using the Theil measure of inequality, it shows that the interregional inequality was high in the 1997–1998 periods but declined subsequently. Moreover, the richer regions did not grow more rapidly with the recovery nor did households in richer regions increase their consumption more rapidly than those in poorer regions. Within-region inequality accounts for most of the inequality in Russia. About 10% of aggregate inequality in consumption in the Russian Federation can be attributed to interregional inequality, while the remaining 90% is due to within-region inequality. The implication is that federal policies should encourage regions to monitor and develop policies to keep the within-region inequality in check. However, given the relatively large differences in socioeconomic conditions, it is important to continue the continuous monitoring and addressing of regional differences. There are also large regional differences in the incidence of poverty. The headcount ratio varied in 2002 between 3.1% and 55.6%. While some of these differences are attributed to different characteristics of the regions in terms of urbanization, education, and employment, large regional differences continue even when these characteristics are accounted for. Persons with the same characteristics are three times more likely to be poor in the Dagestan oblast[10] or in Tuva Republic compared with persons in the rich Tumen oblast or in Moscow City.

As regards WTO accession, the study shows that tariff reduction would lead to significant gains, yielding 1.3 percentage points of improvement in consumption. Tariff reduction should lead to improved allocation of resources in Russia, as resources will be induced to shift to sectors where they are more highly valued at world prices. More important, tariff reduction would more readily permit Russian businesses to import products that contain new and diverse technologies. This would lead to productivity gains. But the Russian tariff is at present not very high (1.6% of GDP or about 7% of the value of import). Therefore, this would not yield the largest macroeconomic effect, although it would be important for a few sectors. Liberalization of the barriers to FDI in the services sectors is the most important source of gains from WTO accession. About 5.3 percentage points of the estimated increase in consumption would follow from liberalization of the barriers to multinational providers of services. Examples of the barriers that are under negotiation as part of the WTO accession are as follows: the monopoly on long distance telephone services; the restraints on multinational banks opening affiliates in Russia; and the quotas on multinational providers of insurance services. Russian commitments to multinational service providers would encourage more FDI in Russia. This would give Russian businesses improved access to the services of multinational service providers in such sectors as telecommunications, banking,

---

[10] Russian Federation is divided into 47 oblasts or provinces.

insurance, and transportation. This should lower the cost of doing business and should also lead to productivity gains for firms using these services.

2.3. India

After the British left in 1947, India decided to establish a democratic form of government with a federal structure and never deviated from the democratic path except for a short period of time, between June 1975 and January 1977, during which period Prime Minister Mrs Indira Gandhi declared internal emergency that involved a suspension of the constitution. So far as the structure of the economy is concerned, the choice was made in favor of a mixed economy in which a government-owned public sector dominated the private sector that was strictly regulated by a complex system of industrial licensing and import permits. The first five-year plan, which started in 1951–1952, and the subsequent five-year plans set the direction of the economy, and the private sector was driven in that direction. All private undertakings, with fewer than 50 workers using power or fewer than 100 workers and not using power, were subjected to industrial licensing, whose purpose was to achieve the pattern of industrialization envisaged in the five-year plans. In 1969, the Government of India nationalized all banks whose nationwide deposits exceeded 500 million Indian rupees. The government's objective of nationalization of general insurance was achieved in 1972 by setting up General Insurance Corporation that functioned as a government monopoly. During early 1970s, India established a repressive foreign investment regime with all projects involving more than 40% foreign equity requiring cabinet approval, which transmitted a clear negative signal to foreign investors. Equally restrictive was the foreign trade policy. By 1970–1971, an elaborate system of import control and export subsidies was in full force. Import licensing covered all imports and foreign exchange allocation to importers was strictly regulated with almost all consumer goods excluded from the list of products that could be imported. An amendment to the Industrial Disputes Act of 1947 made it virtually impossible for large companies employing 100 workers or more to lay-off workers, resulting in higher wage demands, loss of labor productivity, and a preference for capital intensive industries. The Urban Land Ceiling Act of 1976 fixed a ceiling of 500 to $2,000 \, \text{m}^2$ land that can be held by a company in an urban area. All these policies led to what is often referred to as "strangulation of industry" (Panagariya, 2008).

Among the main objectives of the planning process was to establish a socialistic pattern of society, in the pursuit of which the Government of India introduced progressive taxation with very high marginal income tax rates. The percentage of tax revenue accruing to the center and the states increased from 8.3% of GDP in 1960–1961 to 16.5% in 1985–1986 (Thimmaiah, 2002). The percentage annual rate of growth of gross domestic investment in India was 5.6% during 1960–1970, and the gross domestic savings rate was about 14% at the beginning of this period (*World Development Report*, 1979), which increased only marginally during 1980s to about 18% (Panagariya, 2008). Income growth rate in India, prior to 1980s, is stated to be abysmally low at 1% per annum and often referred to as the Hindu rate of growth, which increased to 3.7% during 1980s. The so-called Hindu growth rate was perhaps an underestimate, while annual growth rates had tremendous fluctuations during 1951–1980, with negative growth rates reported in many years. Official poverty measure in term of headcount ratio was more than 50% during 1970s and decreased to an average of about 40% during 1980s (Bhalla, 2002). However, inequality in household income distribution, measured by Gini index, went up from 0.416 in 1975–1976 to 0.425 in 1994–1995 (Bhalla and Vashishtha, 1988). In a study on interregional inequality in India, Das and Barua (1996) have shown that during 1970–1992, inequality among Indian states has increased in almost every sphere of economic activity, particularly in the unorganized industry, which is indirectly supported by Aiyar (2001), who shows that Indian states are converging to different steady states that are determined partly by their respective literacy rates and private investment.

In an interesting approach, Panagariya (2008) has identified four phases of Indian economic experience, each phase representing a policy regime.

Phase I: 1951–1965, with an annual average growth rate of 4.1%.
Phase II: 1965–1981, with an annual average growth rate of 3.2%.
Phase III: 1981–1988, with an annual average growth rate of 4.8%.
Phase IV: 1988–present time, with an annual average growth rate of 6.3% during 1988–2006.

Even though the basic structure of the mixed economy was established in phase I, government policy was less interventionist in this phase than in the next phase. However, the first Prime Minister, Mr Jawaharlal Nehru, whose foreign policy was designed in accordance with nonalignment, was in favor of autarky that is to be achieved through economic planning rather than by restrictive trade policies. According to Bhagwati and Desai (1970), the period of the first five-year plan (1951–1956) was one of progressive liberalization and import-GDP ratio shows a slight increase in the trend during the plan period. Even foreign investment policy was open and liberal, with national treatment accorded to existing foreign enterprises. However, the industrial policy regime was restrictive in phase I. It had three objectives: to establish a dominant role of the public sector in heavy industries; to regulate private business through licensing; and to introduce a system of public distribution of goods and price control. Nehru's focus on industry resulted in a neglect of agriculture in setting plan priorities. No major institutional change in agriculture, such as land reform, was envisaged. The farmers were subjected to price disincentives with the Essential Commodities Act of 1955, which effectively put price ceilings on commodities of essential consumption.

Phase II may be characterized by political instability and wars with Pakistan in 1965 and 1971, the latter resulting in huge influx of refugees from Bangladesh. Mr Lal Bahadur Shastri, who succeeded Mr Nehru in 1964, wanted to change the emphasis from heavy industry to agriculture and, in fact, laid the foundation of Green Revolution, which stands for use of genetically modified high-yield seeds to raise land productivity. Unfortunately, Mr Shastri passed away in January 1966 and Mrs Indira Gandhi, who succeeded him, had to face internal power struggle within the Congress Party. For political survival, she moved toward the left of center and was responsible for highly restrictive foreign trade and investment regimes and an interventionist industrial policy, as already mentioned. During this phase of the Indian economy, many East Asian countries, such as South Korea and Taiwan, took advantage of a favorable world market environment and adopted outward-looking policies that resulted in high rates of growth. India, however, went further inward, with import-GDP ratio plunging below 4% during 1969–1973, compared to an average of more than 6% in phase I. Agriculture, which was neglected in phase I, now started to drag the economy down. Between 1965 and 1981, agriculture, forestry, and fishing had negative growth rates in 8 of 16 years. The trend growth rates during 1965–1981 were, respectively, 2.1%, 4.0%, 3.9%, and 4.3% in agriculture, industry, manufacturing, and services, while GDP rate grew at 3.2%. The failure of economic policy culminated in Emergency Rule in 1975 and Mrs Gandhi lost the elections in 1977. Political instability continued with a non-Congress Party coalition government, until Mrs Gandhi's resounding election victory in 1980. However, she was assassinated in 1984 and her son Mr Rajiv Gandhi became the Prime Minister, who was subsequently assassinated in 1991. There are, however, two positive features in phase II. First, the effect of Green Revolution finally kicked in. Though there were many negative annual growth rates of agricultural production during this phase, the trend growth rate of net production of food grains (net production = gross production − 12.5% for seed and waste) was positive. Second, gross savings rate climbed from 12% in the first half of 1960s to 18% in mid-1970s and to 21% by late 1970s. Investment as a percentage of GDP increased from 4.9% in 1964–1965 to 9.7% in 1980–1981. However, the corporate sector investment as a percentage in GDP fell during the same period, as the government absorbed most of the increase in household savings.

Phase III, which is known as "liberalization by stealth", may be characterized by piecemeal and limited liberalization of industry and trade, raising import-GDP ratio from an average of about 6% in 1970s to about 7.5% in 1980s. Foreign investment and technology import were also liberalized to some extent. However, this limited liberalization increased growth rate to 5.6% in 1981–1991 which compares quite well with the growth rate of 5.8% in 1991–2001 that was achieved after the introduction of major economic reforms in 1991.

Phase IV began with a high rate of growth causing a balance of payment crisis that forced India to borrow from IMF and accept the conditionality attached to the loan. After the assassination of Mr Rajiv Gandhi, the coalition government headed by Mr Narasimha Rao appointed Dr Manmohan Singh as the Finance Minister, who reformed industrial policy, foreign investment policy in 1991 and substantially reduced tariff rates. Import licensing of capital goods and intermediate goods was scrapped to correct the overvaluation of the exchange rate. The growth rate achieved during

1993–1997 was 7.1%, along with about a 10% hike in the consumer price index. The Congress Party lost the election in 1996 mainly due to high inflation and corruption issues; this marked the end of era in Indian politics that was almost completely dominated by the party. None of the subsequent governments had a clear majority and had to form coalition with other parties. Fortunately, none of these coalition governments rolled back the economic reform measures introduced in 1991, and Indian economy was progressively integrated with the world economy in this phase, with exports doubling in just three years and export of goods and services as a percentage of GDP reaching 20.5% in 2005–2006 from 11.6% in 1999–2000.

The current view on India's growth spurt makes a distinction between the Indian model and the East Asian model (Kotwal *et al.*, 2011). According to this approach, Indian economic growth during the last three decades was not caused by high domestic savings or foreign capital inflow or manufacturing export and it was certainly not state-driven. The important factors behind this growth experience are cheaper and easier access to imported technology, improved telecommunication system, increased usage of internet, availability of a diverse set of skills developed during the phase of import substitution, and continuity of the predominant role of agriculture in providing employment that has led to substantial reduction in rural poverty. While the manufacturing sector was the major source of growth in East and Southeast Asia, in India's case, it was the service sector and software export.

Some of the studies dealing with economic growth and poverty reduction in India, such as Dutt and Ravallion (2002), suggest that India has probably maintained its 1980s rate of poverty reduction in the 1990s. The incidence of poverty has been falling at a little less than one percentage point per year over the main post-reform period. However, the basic question of measuring India's poverty rate has turned out to be harder to answer than it needed to be because of difficulties with coverage and comparability of the survey data. The impact of greater openness of the Indian economy achieved by the economic reforms introduced in 1991 on growth–poverty–inequality triangle has been studied by Biswas and Sindzingre (2006) and their main findings are as follows. Neither solely inward looking (import substitution) nor solely outward-oriented trade policies (export promotion) can be said to have a positive impact on alleviating poverty at the state level in the face of increasing overall openness. Rather, it has been found that given the composition of India's trade, an admixture of export-promotion and import-substitution policies can help a state manage its poverty better, rather than a solely inward- or outward- looking policy, since the states that have adopted either of these two (or both) policies have done better in poverty management compared to the others. Poverty is a multidimensional concept. This is especially true for a country like India where social stratification remains extremely resilient. Therefore, it does not make much sense to claim that a single factor has affected poverty and run regressions to measure the extent of that. For example, some studies estimate the elasticity of poverty, measured by headcount ratio, with respect growth rates or other factors. As regards the view that during the entire liberalization period poverty decline has suffered a setback and inequality has increased, this study claims that increasing openness may or may not make a state more vulnerable vis-à-vis its poverty management.

A similar view is expressed by Ghosh (2010). The Indian Planning Commission data show that there has been a setback in the rate of poverty reduction in the post-liberalization period. This is shown in Table 2.7.

According to Ghosh (2010), India, with its market-driven and demand-constrained system, has not only failed in delivering a growth success that is comparable to China but also been far less successful with poverty reduction. Clearly, macroeconomic flexibility in a market-driven environment is not the best recipe either for growth and stability or for poverty reduction. India's growth experience, while better than for many other developing

Table 2.7. Annual percentage rates of poverty reduction in India.

Period	Rural	Urban
1973–1988	−1.24 (−2.19)[a]	−0.79 (−1.60)[a]
1988–2005	−0.64 (−1.62)[a]	−0.74 (−1.92)[a]

[a]Normalized to initial year.
Source: Planning Commission, Government of India.

countries, was still less than the rapid growth experienced by China and other East and Southeast Asian economies. And more fundamentally, it could not deliver the desired structural change in terms of the composition of output and employment that would have ensured substantial poverty reduction. These inadequacies of the recent growth process in India are related to the reduced public expenditure by the Indian state in the period of reform, most significantly the substantial reduction in central capital expenditure (mainly on infrastructure) as a share of GDP and also public expenditure directed toward rural areas generally. In addition, central government policies created resource problems for the state governments in various ways, forcing them to cut back on crucial developmental expenditure. This meant that first, rates of aggregate income growth were well below those which could have been achieved and, second, that employment growth was well below the rate of GDP growth. These problems were compounded by the effects that trade liberalization had on small-scale production in some manufacturing sectors. Agrarian distress and inadequate employment generation have thus emerged as the most significant macroeconomic problems currently faced by the Indian economy.

Some of the conclusions of these studies indicate that India may not be able to sustain a high growth phase along with steady rates of poverty reduction in the long run, partly due to adverse structural changes but mostly due to slow growth in infrastructure spending. Even a cursory look at National Accounts Statistics (NAS) would reveal that the share of electricity, gas, and water supply plus construction accounts for roughly 10% of GDP and this has not significantly changed from 2004 to 2010. Infrastructure may turn into a bottleneck not only because its rate of growth is less than what is desirable but also due to its poor quality. The main provider of social capital in India is the government. There are allegations of widespread corruption in government-funded public works programs both at the central and state government levels (see Das, 2010), which results in a poor quality of social capital. The second most important reason to be skeptical about the sustainability of India's growth process is its foreign investment policy. Das and Pant (2006) have made a survey of current incentives offered to foreign investors in South Asia. India has liberalized foreign investment policy in successive steps starting from 1991. Even then, India has not been able to attract foreign investment at a scale that is comparable to China. Among many reasons, the two most important ones may be the poor quality of infrastructure and a lack of transparency in government policy related to approval of foreign investment projects.

2.4. China

China was never exactly a British colony like India, which in its early phase of colonization, was ruled by a British company called the East India Company. From its base in India, the Company had also been engaged in an increasingly profitable opium export trade to China since the 1730s. This trade, illegal in China, since it was outlawed by the Qing dynasty in 1729, helped reverse the trade imbalances resulting from the British imports of tea, which saw large outflows of silver from Britain to China.[11] In 1839, the confiscation by the Chinese authorities at Canton of 20,000 chests of opium led Britain to attack China in the First Opium War and resulted in the seizure of Hong Kong Island by Britain — at that time a minor settlement.[12]

The history of modern China begins with the establishment of the People's Republic of China. Following the Chinese Civil War and the victory of Mao Zedong's Communist forces over the Kuomintang forces of Generalissimo Chiang Kai-shek, who fled to Taiwan, Mao declared the founding of the People's Republic of China on October 1, 1949. Mao's first goal was a total overhaul of the land ownership system and extensive land reforms. China's old system of landlord ownership of farmland and tenant peasants was replaced with a distribution system in favor of poor/landless peasants. Mao laid heavy emphasis on class struggle and theoretical work and in 1953 began various campaigns to persecute former landlords and merchants, including the execution of more powerful landlords. Drug trafficking in the country as well as foreign investment were largely wiped out. Many buildings of historical and cultural significance as well as countless artifacts were destroyed by the Maoist regime, since they were considered reminders of the "feudal" past.

---

[11] Martin (2007).
[12] Janin (1999).

The economic policy regime of modern China can be divided into the Mao Zedong era (1949–1976) and Deng Xiaoping era (1979–1997).[13] The 27 years of the Mao era were marked by the Great Leap Forward (1958–1960) and the Cultural Revolution (1966–1976). The Great Leap Forward will be remembered for its crude or traditional Chinese technologies and mass mobilization of labor, resulting in policy mistakes, natural disasters, extreme food shortages, and deaths due to starvation. Following the turmoil of the Cultural Revolution, China launched, in 1978, four modernization programs for agriculture, industry, national defense, and science and technology.[14] After the first set of reforms proved successful in the rural areas, reforms were vigorously implemented in the urban areas from 1984. Since China witnessed frequent regime changes, it is useful to keep track of the periods of policy changes:

(1) 1949–1952: The beginning of a socialist economy and land redistribution.
(2) 1952–1956: The Cooperative Movement.
(3) 1956–1958: The Communization Movement.
(4) 1958–1961: The Great Leap Forward, which followed the Soviet model of heavy industrialization neglecting light industry and agriculture.
(5) 1961–1966: A period of economic recovery.
(6) 1966–1976: The Cultural Revolution during which economic progress was stalled.
(7) 1984–present day: Market-oriented reforms.

When China functioned as a centrally planned economy, decisions concerning consumption, distribution, and investment were determined by state. Pricing policy set the terms of trade with the objective of mobilizing resources to the state sector. Persistent shortages arose even after controlling household incomes.[15] During the first five-year plan, launched in 1953, SOEs were administered by 20 ministries in the State Council. The

[13] Yabuki and Harner (1999).
[14] Yueh (2010) and Riskin (1987).
[15] Kornai (1992).

first plan created a large-scale capital-intensive producer goods industry. The problems of coordination, control, and incentives led to a push for decentralization, particularly after Soviet credit dried up in 1955. However, decentralization resulted in sectoral imbalances and centralization returned with the Great Leap Forward in 1957–1958. By 1961, centralized planning was restored. Disastrous effects of the Great Leap Forward during 1963–1965 marked a period of readjustment and recovery. Industrial policy started to focus on investment in a small number of priority sectors. Agriculture and foreign trade became priorities. But all this ended with the Cultural Revolution in 1966.

In the early 1950s, land was confiscated from the landlords and redistributed. Chairman Mao reorganized cooperatives into communes where land was collectively owned by the members. By 1979, 88% of all rural households were organized into cooperatives or collectives. In 1979, there were 53,300 communes, divided into 669,000 brigades and 5.14 million production teams or villages (Yueh, 2010). Between 1958 and 1978, some farmers had small, private plots and some rural markets existed.

The inward-looking character of the Chinese economy during 1952–1974 becomes evident, as export plus import as a percentage of GDP averaged about 6% during this period. In the 1960s, after the break with the former Soviet Union, trade stagnated. China turned outward in the 1970s. The real value of trade with non-centrally planned economies grew by 78% during 1970–1973. Economic performance in China was poor, compared to other East Asian countries, such as Japan and South Korea. With Mao's death, the Communist Party of China leadership turned to market-oriented reforms to salvage the failing economy (Brandt et al., 2008). Economic reforms began after Deng Xiaoping and his reformist allies ousted the Gang of Four Maoist faction. By the time Deng took power, there was widespread support among the elite for economic reforms. As *de facto* leader, Deng's policies faced opposition from party conservatives but were extremely successful in increasing the country's wealth. Deng's reform started with agriculture, long neglected by the communist party. By the late 1970s, food supplies and production had become so deficient that government officials were warning that China was about to repeat the "disaster of 1959" — the famines which killed tens of millions during the Great Leap Forward (Brandt et al., 2008). The process of decollectivization of agriculture divided the land of the People's Communes into private plots. Farmers were able to keep the land's output after paying a share to the state. This move increased agricultural production and the living standards of hundreds of millions of farmers and stimulated rural industry. Reforms were also implemented in urban industry to increase productivity. A dual price system was introduced, in which state-owned industries were allowed to sell any production above the plan quota, and commodities were sold at both plan and market prices, allowing citizens to avoid the shortages of the Maoist era. Private businesses were allowed to operate for the first time since the Communist takeover, and they gradually began to make up a greater percentage of industrial output. Price flexibility was also increased, expanding the service sector (Brandt *et al.*, 2008). Deng created a series of special economic zones for foreign investment that was relatively free of the bureaucratic regulations and interventions that hampered economic growth. These regions became engines of growth for the national economy.

The period between 1984 and 1993 is marked by over-privatization of SOEs, resulting in opposition of reforms from conservative leaders whose vested interest was threatened by loss of bureaucratic control. Conservative elder opposition, led by Chen Yun, prevented many major reforms which would have damaged the interests of special interest groups in the government bureaucracy. Corruption and high rates of inflation led to widespread discontent, contributing to the Tiananmen Square protests of 1989. However, Deng stood by his reforms and, in 1992, affirmed the need to continue reforms in his southern tour. He also reopened the Shanghai Stock Exchange closed by Mao 40 years earlier (Naughton, 2008). Even though the economy grew reasonably fast and established the foundation of the socialist market economy, the state sector incurred heavy losses that had to be made up from state revenues. In the 1990s, Deng forced many of the conservative elders like Chen Yun into retirement, allowing radical reforms to be carried out. Despite Deng's death in 1997, reforms continued under his handpicked successors, Jiang Zemin and Zhu Rongii, who were ardent reformers. In 1997 and 1998, large-scale privatization occurred, in which all state enterprises, except a few large monopolies, were liquidated and their assets sold to private investors. Between 2001 and 2004, the number of SOEs decreased by 48% (Rawski *et al.*, 2008). During the same period, Jiang and Zhu also reduced tariffs, trade barriers and regulations, reformed the banking system, dismantled much of the Mao-era social welfare system, forced the People's Liberation Army to divest itself of military-run businesses, reduced inflation, and joined the WTO. These moves invoked discontent among some groups — especially the laid-off workers of privatized state enterprises. The domestic private sector first exceeded 50% of GDP in 2005 and has further expanded since. However, some state monopolies still remained, such as in petroleum and banking.

The conservative Hu-Wen administration began to reverse some of Deng Xiaoping's reforms in 2005. More egalitarian and populist policies resulted in increased subsidies and tighter control over the healthcare sector. An easy money policy led to United States-style property bubble and the property values tripled. The privileged state sector was flooded with government investment with the idea that they could compete with foreign multinational corporations (Naughton, 2008). Economists estimate China's GDP growth from 1978 to 2005 at 9.5% a year. Since the beginning of Deng Xiaoping's reforms, China's GDP has risen tenfold. Per capita incomes grew at 6.6% per year (Herston *et al.*, 2008).

There has been a great deal of research to explain the success of the Chinese experiment in moving from the planned economy to the socialist market economy. First, the decentralization of state authority allowed the local leaders to experiment with various ways to privatize the state sector and energize the economy (Brandt *et al.*, 2008). Second, the provincial governments in China were hungry for investment and competition among them reduced regulations and barriers to investment. Third, China's success was also due to the export-led growth strategy followed by Four Asian Tigers (Sharma, 2007). Fourth, the collapse of the Soviet Bloc created an impetus to reform the economy in a different course, avoiding the Russian experiment with market capitalism that resulted in the rise of powerful oligarchs, corruption, and loss of state revenues (Remnick, 1997). The latest work on this issue by Song *et al.* (2011) is based on a growth model consistent with China's high output growth, sustained returns on capital, reallocation within the manufacturing sector, and a large trade surplus. The main findings are as follows. China's entrepreneurial firms use more productive technologies than state-owned firms but depend mainly on internal savings for financing investment. The state-owned firms have low productivity but a preferential access to credit markets that the entrepreneurial firms do not have. The high productivity firms outgrow the low productivity firms if they have high savings. The low productivity firms that are state-owned thrive partly due to the credit market imperfection. The downsizing of financially integrated domestic private enterprises forces domestic savings to be invested abroad, generating a trade surplus, which is simply a result of structural imperfection. The study argues against the view that the Chinese government keeps currency value artificially low to generate the trade surplus; as such a policy would trigger an adjustment of real exchange rate through inflation, which is not visible.

Economic reforms have virtually eliminated poverty in urban China and substantially reduced it in rural areas. Between 1993 and 2008, extreme poverty declined from 55% to about 16% (Arnal and Förster, 2010). However, economic disparity has grown during the post-reform years. The Gini measure of inequality of 0.45 would be considered high by any standard. Increased inequality may have been caused by the disappearance of the welfare state. Income disparity between the coastal and interior provinces may be explained by the fact that the latter is burdened by a larger state sector. The revival of the welfare state and a progressive income tax system designed to redistribute income may reduce inequality (Benjamin *et al.*, 2008). There is, however, no clear consensus on the magnitude of interprovincial inequality in China. Rui and Zheng (2009) have shown that consumption-based measures indicate low interprovincial inequality, whereas a strong upward trend is observed, when using GDP per worker. Moreover, most interprovincial inequality results from intraprovincial inequality due to the rural-urban divide in each province.

In the mid-1990s, China introduced a progressive market reform that dealt with both the restructuring of SOEs — allowing them to recruit workers without planning permission — and the substitution of life-time employment by indefinite and temporary labor contracts, as provided in the 1994 Labor Law. As a result, at the end of the 1990s, four million jobs were lost per year due to the restructuring of the SOEs. Chinese official statistics shows an increase in the urban registered unemployment rate from 2% to 4.2% between 1990 and 2008. However, this rate is not comparable to international standards. To be comparable, data have to be estimated from the annual labor force surveys, whose questions correspond to the job-search categories used internationally. These surveys provide data for total employment as well as the number of the economically active population, and unemployment is then calculated as the difference between the two. Following this method, it has been estimated that the unemployment rate of the urban working population, excluding those working in agriculture, peaked in 2000 at nearly 10% and slowly decreased thereafter to reach levels of around 6% in 2008 (OECD, 2010a,b). Cai *et al.* (2009) point to similar results, showing clearly that the unemployment level in China is higher than official statistics suggest.

However, employment in agriculture remains about 40% of workforce in China (Arnal and Förster, 2010), compared to less than 5% in the Organisation for Economic Co-operation and Development (OECD) countries. Indeed, China and India are still characterized by a large excess of labor in rural areas. Whereas four in five workers in India are found in rural areas, in China the ratio is almost two-third, which gives an estimated labor surplus of around 170 million workers in China and 130 million in India (OECD, 2007).

There is evidence that market-oriented reform has probably reduced regional economic imbalances in China during the 1990s. Jian *et al.* (1996) have examined the tendency toward convergence in real per-capita income among the provinces of China during the period 1952–1993. Real incomes in Chinese provinces did not display strong convergence or divergence during the initial phase of central planning, 1952–1965. During the Cultural Revolution, 1965–1978, regional inequality widened, as Socialist planning favored the already richer industrial regions at the expense of the poorer agricultural regions. It was only after market-oriented reforms began in 1978 that regional incomes began to equalize sharply. This convergence was strongly associated with the rise in rural productivity and was particularly strong within the group of provinces that were allowed to integrate with the outside world. Starting in 1990, although convergence continued within these coastal provinces, they had started to grow markedly faster than the interior, and thus regional incomes had started to diverge once again. This study has estimated the β-convergence coefficients for a core group of 15 Chinese provinces for the entire period and 28 provinces in the post-reform period. The β-convergence coefficients are coefficients

Table 2.8.   Convergence regression for China.

	1952–1965	1965–1978	1978–1993
Constant	0.008	0.103	−0.004
	(0.302)	(6.137)	(0.237)
Log of initial per capita real GDP	−0.006	0.016	−0.017
	(−1.126)	(3.375)	(−3.320)
Number of provinces	15	15	28
R-squared	0.088	0.518	0.298

Source: Jian *et al.* (1996), p. 8.

of a regression of annual growth rates of real GDP on initial per capita real GDP, which are produced in Table 2.8, where a positive coefficient indicates divergence and a negative coefficient shows convergence.

A recent study on China's regional inequality by Keidel (2009) reveals rural income and consumption divergence for both 1980–2005 and 2000–2005 for seven provinces. But while real rural consumption growth averaged 7.7% over 1985–2005 in the eastern coastal region, it averaged 6.5% uniformly in the interior. But the study suggests that higher regional inequality and accompanying interregional migration indicate that inequality plays an important positive role in inducing economic actors to voluntarily move to more productive locations and activities as a mechanism for ensuring sustainable improvements in individual well-being.

CHAPTER 3

Economic Growth, Income Inequality, and Poverty

Income distribution can be solely determined by the state in a command economy along with a plan to achieve high rates of economic growth. The former Soviet Union, particularly under the leadership of Stalin, had planned to achieve high rates of industrialization without regard for its implications for poverty. However, with a command economy system, Soviet Union never had a situation of high income inequality. With the end of the Cold War era, markets took over the role of allocator of resources even in China, where the Communist Party is in power. What one may learn from standard economic theory is that if the markets are perfectly competitive and there is no government intervention, market will achieve the most efficient allocation of resources and take the economy toward the optimal growth path. The standard theory is silent on the question whether economic growth will be at the cost of higher income inequality. But in a market economy, growth is generally believed to cause income inequalities at least at some stages of economic development. The literature dealing with growth and income distribution is fairly diversified, as it includes theoretical issues, country experiences, and econometric modeling of processes that are related with growth, poverty, and income distribution. It will be sufficient to cite a few key studies such as Kuznets (1955) and Williamson (1965) for the "inverted-U" hypothesis; Kakwani (1986), Bhatty (1974), and Jain and Tendulkar (1990) for country studies; and Das and Barua (1996) and Ravallion and Datt (1990) for econometric modeling. The inverted-U hypothesis of Simon Kuznets has been widely discussed in development literature and it directly addresses the relationship between economic growth and income inequality. The nature of this relationship depends of the country's initial per capita income; countries with low per capita income are likely to face rising inequality, while the countries with

Table 3.1.   Income and inequality in selected countries.

Country	Income per capita (US$, 2008)	Gini coefficient	Survey year
Low income			
Ethiopia	280	29.8	2005
Mozambique	380	47.1	2003
Nepal	400	47.3	2004
Cambodia	640	40.7	2007
Zambia	950	50.7	2005
Lower middle income			
India	1,040	36.8	2005
Cameroon	1,150	44.6	2001
Bolivia	1,460	57.2	2007
Egypt	1,800	32.1	2005
Indonesia	1,880	37.6	2007
Upper middle income			
Namibia	4,210	74.3	1993
Bulgaria	5,490	29.2	2003
South Africa	5,820	57.8	2000
Argentina	7,190	48.8	2006
Brazil	7,300	55.0	2007
Mexico	9,990	51.6	2008
Upper income			
Hungary	12,810	30.0	2004
Spain	31,930	34.7	2000
Germany	42,710	28.3	2000
United States	47,930	40.8	2000
Norway	87,340	25.8	2000

Source: Quoted from Todaro and Smith (2012).

sufficiently high per capita income will be able to reduce income inequality in the process of economic growth. International data on per capita incomes and personal income inequality measured by Gini coefficient roughly support this hypothesis, as Table 3.1 shows that income inequality reaches the highest values for the upper middle income countries.

3.1.   Growth Models and Growth–Inequality Relationship

The theoretical relationship between economic growth and income distribution generally turns out to be a complex one. It will be prudent to look at the theoretical models of economic growth to find out if there is any discussion on growth and income distribution. The so-called Cambridge models of Kaldor (1956) and Pasinetti (1974) discuss the relationship between growth and distribution in the framework of equilibrium growth. Economic growth is the result of household savings being invested in expanding production capacity. Two important parameters in these models are the workers' and the capitalists' propensities to save. In Kaldor's model, equilibrium is attained if the warranted rate of growth of income, which is the ratio between the average of the two savings propensities (s) and the incremental capital output ratio (v), is equal to the natural rate of growth which, in the absence of any technological change, is the exogenously determined rate of population growth. In steady state, the per capita income stops growing and its value is determined in such a way that s/v is equal to the rate of growth of population. If per capita income happens to exceed its steady-state value, then the actual growth rate of income ($\Delta Y/Y$) will be less than s/v, which also means that $\Delta Y/Y$ is less than the rate of population growth resulting in a fall in the per capita income. In the process of income contraction, investment ($v\Delta Y$) falls short of total savings (sY) which, under the condition of full employment, will lead to a fall in the price level and a rise in the real wage rate as well as the share of wages in national income. Thus, the decline in per capita income in the adjustment process is associated with an improvement in the income distribution. Conversely, if per capita income is less than its steady-state value, investment will exceed total savings, the price level and the share of profit in national income will rise, as per capita income rises to approach its steady-state value. Both Kaldor and Pasinetti, particularly the latter, insisted on the irrelevance of workers' propensity to save. But the overall relationship between the growth of income and the extent of equality in the distribution of income between wage earners and capitalists is a negative one. Another important aspect of Cambridge growth models as well as the neoclassical growth models is that in the process of income redistribution the real rewards going to the various economic classes do not remain constant. All these models keep government out of the picture and do not deal with the redistribution policies and their possible moderating effect on income distribution that may move in the adverse direction in the process of economic growth.

Both in the Cambridge models and the neoclassical models, one finds a relationship between growth and distribution only when the economy is off the steady-state path. If one assumes that the economy is always on the steady-state path, the rate of growth of income is determined by the exogenously given rate of growth of population with no change in income distribution as neither the factor shares nor the real returns to factors change. An introduction of technological change will, however, change all this because it may cause a shift in the steady-state path of income growth. Technological progress will also change income distribution even if it is of the Hicks-neutral type. The effect of technological progress on growth is unquestionably positive, but its effect on income distribution depends on the nature of the technological progress. For instance, a technological progress occurring in the capital-intensive industry may change income distribution in favor of capital.

Most of the recent theoretical works on growth and income distribution, such as Loury (1981) and Banerjee and Newman (1991), emphasize the role of certain initial conditions. Galor and Zeira (1993) have shown that in the presence of capital market imperfections and indivisibilities in investment in human capital, the initial distribution of wealth affects aggregate output and investment in both the short and long run, as there are multiple steady states.

The subsequent work on income distribution and growth has become a part of development economics with the contributions of Kuznets (1955) and Williamson (1965) who have built both the conceptual and empirical basis of the "inverted- U hypothesis." Recently, there has been a revival of interest in the relationship between growth and distribution. Persson and Tabellini (1994) have used an overlapping generation model to show that a reduction of income inequality raises the growth rate of income, assuming that the median income class in the population makes all the political decisions relating to income transfers that are uniform. An income transfer is defined as uniform if income is transferred from the above average to below average earners in proportion to the difference between the income earned and average income. They implicitly assume that the median income exceeds the arithmetic mean, which implies that the income distribution is negatively skewed with the longer tail falling on the lower range of income. The median class will vote for a transfer if and only if the transfer does not curtail their incentive to accumulate more productive assets. Since by definition, a transfer will benefit at least 50% of the population who would accumulate more productive assets, one tautologically gets a positive relationship between growth and equity. The model simply provides an alternative explanation of the forces behind the falling segment of the inverted-U curve, where there is no conflict between growth and reduction of income inequality. However, the most restrictive assumption of this model is the constancy of the rate of return accruing to the asset holders in the process of income transfers.

Das (2005) has combined the idea of uniform income transfer in Persson and Tabellini (1994) with a growth process driven by accumulation. A few extensions of this formulation can be made to show that growth necessarily leads to income convergence in the class of below average earners and may cause income divergence in the class of above average earners. In a highly unequal income distribution, the number of below average earners will exceed that of above average earners by a big margin. Thus, higher the inequality in income distribution, the greater is the possibility of economic growth causing a reduction in inequality. This adds a new dimension to the Kuznets–Williamson thesis. Whether income inequality rises at low levels of per capita income or not depends on the initial level of inequality. If the level of inequality is high at low per capita incomes, growth may reduce inequality if uniform income transfers take place. On the other hand, growth may increase inequality even at high per capita incomes, if the initial distribution is not very unequal.

3.2. Inequality Measures

Before modeling the dynamic relationship between income growth and income inequality, it is necessary to look at some of the empirical measures of income inequality and understand how these measures operate at different levels of disaggregation. The two most popular inequality measures that have been used in empirical studies are the Theil entropy index and the Gini coefficient. There are many ways in which economic inequality can be measured and the index of inequality that one uses depends largely on the context. If we are interested in the inequality among regions/states of a federal economy, then it is necessary to compare one region's shares in country's income and population with those of the other regions. If, for instance, it turns out that a single region having only 5% of the country's population accounts for 50% of its income, then the regional inequality must be considered rather acute. If, on the other hand, for most regions, the share in population and the share in the country's income are close, then inequality is not very large. Theil's (1967) entropy measure is defined in the following way. Let y_k be the share of the kth region in the country's gross national product (GNP) and p_k its share in the total population $(k = 1, 2, \ldots, K)$. Then an absolute equality in the regional distribution of income is represented by a situation in which the ratio, y_k/p_k is unity for all regions. Any deviation of this ratio from unity indicates inequality which is measured by T_Y:

$$T_Y = \sum_{k=1}^{K} y_k \log (y_k/p_k), \qquad (3.1)$$

where K is the total number of states/regions and $\sum y_k = \sum p_k = 1$. The ratio between the kth state's income share and population share, that is, y_k/p_k, is nothing but the ratio between its per capita income and the country's per capita income. We may, therefore, designate y_k/p_k as the kth state's relative income. The welfare of the kth state is assumed to be a function of its relative income and let $\log (y_k/p_k)$ be the kth state's welfare function. If income share y_k is taken as the probability of achieving the relative income y_k/p_k, then T_Y is the expected welfare of the kth state. Any increase in T_Y would indicate an increase in interstate inequality. Some terms in T_Y take negative values for states/regions whose income shares are less than their respective population shares. But Theil has given a proof that $T_Y \geq 0$ and we will not repeat it here.

T_Y has a minimum equal to zero which is attained (subject to the condition that the shares add up to unity) when, for all states, the income share and the population share are identical. The situation of maximum interstate inequality arises when, for a given assignment of nonzero population shares to all states, the income share of one state, say the hth state, tends to unity, while the income shares of all other states tend to zero. In this case, T_Y tends to $-\log(p_h) > 0$ which is the maximum value of the measure or maximum inequality.

Our choice of the Theil index, T_Y, as a measure of interstate income inequality is based on the consideration that the measure in Equation (3.1) is decomposable and that, as we shall demonstrate, with uniform income transfers, the overall income inequality in a country as well as the interstate and intrastate inequality move in the same direction.

Let n be the population of the country classified into G groups, with the number of people in the gth group being n_g. Therefore, $n = \sum_{g=1}^{G} n_g$. Let y and p denote income and population shares. A group can be defined as region or income class. Then the decomposition works out as follows:

$$\sum_{i=1}^{n} y_i \log(y_i/p_i) = \sum_{g=1}^{G} y_g \log(y_g/p_g) + \sum_{g=1}^{G} y_g E_g, \qquad (3.2)$$

where

$$E_g = \sum_{k=1}^{n_g} y_{kg} \log(y_{kg}/p_{kg}).$$

The term on the left-hand side is the Theil entropy index of inequality among all people or overall inequality. This is decomposed as a summation of several entropy measures appearing on the right-hand side. The first term on the right-hand side is the measure of inequality between groups, with y_g and p_g denoting the income and population shares of the gth group in national totals. The first term, therefore, measures intergroup inequality. The second term is the weighted average of inequality levels within groups or intragroup inequality. The inequality within the gth group is measured by the entropy E_g. In the expression for E_g, the terms y_{kg} and p_{kg} are the income and the population shares of the kth person in the totals of the gth group. The first term is referred to as a measure of "between inequality", whereas the second term stands for "within inequality". Each E_g is a measure of interpersonal inequality in the gth group. The decomposition in Equation (3.2) looks at inequality in three dimensions: overall inequality, interstate inequality, and interpersonal inequality in each state.

Gini index of inequality is derived from the Lorenz curve and it is based on the area between the diagonal and the Lorenz curve. If the Lorenz curve is represented by the function $L(X)$, where X is percentage of population whose income share is $L(X)$, then the Gini index, G is defined as

$$G = 1 - 2 \int_u^1 L(X) dX.$$

For a population whose incomes $y_i, i = 1, 2, \ldots, n$, are indexed in non-decreasing order $(y_i \leq y_{i+1})$:

$$G = \frac{2 \sum_{i=1}^n i Y_i}{n \sum_{i=1}^n Y_i} - \frac{n+1}{n}. \tag{3.3}$$

G takes the lowest value, zero, when the Lorenz curve coincides with the diagonal signifying absence of income inequality and the highest value, one, when the richest 1% of the population earns all the incomes, leaving nothing for the rest. In the formulation (3.3), $G = 0$, if everyone has the same income. Deaton (1997) has proposed a different measure that gives the highest weight to the lowest income. Equation (3.3), however, is the standard measure of inequality. Similar to Theil index, Gini coefficient is decomposable, as shown by Lambert and Aronson (1993). Let G be the Gini coefficient and let the population subgroups be indexed by $k = 1, 2, \ldots, n$. The decomposition takes the form: $G = G_B + \sum a_k G_k + R$, where G_B is the between-groups Gini coefficient, defined as the one which would be obtained if every income in every subgroup were to be replaced by the relevant subgroup mean, a_k is the product of population share and income share going to subgroup k, G_k is the Gini coefficient for income within subgroup k and R is a residual which is zero if the subgroup income ranges do not overlap.

Just to illustrate how the Theil decomposition works, we have applied Equation (3.2), using intercountry data on 94 countries for the period 1979–1993 that is available from *World Development Report* (WDR) grouping of countries according to per capita income. There are four groups: (i) low-income countries, (ii) middle-income countries, (iii) upper-middle income countries, and (iv) high-income countries. The list of countries is given in WDR tables. The results of the decomposition are given in Table 3.2.

Table 3.2.   Four group decomposition of Theil entropy.

Year	94 Countries	Low income countries	Middle income countries	Upper-middle income countries	High income countries	Four group entropy (between inequality)	(within inequality)
(1)	(2)	(3)	(4)	(5)	(6)	(7)	(8)
1979	42.53	2.54	5.49	1.91	1.41	40.85	1.68
1980	44.73	2.74	4.55	17.95	1.59	41.71	3.03
1982	57.04	1.08	3.14	2.14	11.83	46.63	10.41
1983	44.52	0.85	3.26	2.21	3.74	41.10	3.41
1984	45.67	0.92	4.19	2.30	2.39	43.30	2.37
1985	46.76	0.57	2.83	2.34	2.63	44.25	2.51
1986	57.74	0.61	4.52	2.59	9.02	49.59	8.16
1988	49.74	0.93	3.30	2.41	1.42	48.21	1.53
1990	50.00	0.81	4.17	3.35	0.86	48.83	1.17
1991	53.63	8.34	3.42	19.40	1.01	50.91	2.72
1992	51.00	2.33	4.66	6.25	2.84	47.81	3.19
1993	51.22	1.48	6.63	6.24	1.92	48.74	2.48

Source: World Development Reports.

The second column of the table gives the entropy index of inequality among 94 countries. Columns (3) to (6) provide the measures of inequality within each of the four groups of countries. A weighted average of these "within inequalities" is reported in column (8). The weights used are the shares of the respective groups in world's GDP as in the decomposition model presented above. Column 7 gives the index of inequality between the four groups. The decomposition ensures that the sum of columns (7) and (8) is column (2). The values of all entropies are multiplied by 100 for visual convenience. The arithmetic decomposition of the Theil index or the Gini coefficient can identify the major sources of income inequality. Perhaps a better way would be to regress a global income inequality measure on the inequality measures for the components in a Cobb–Douglas framework where the exponents add to unity. We have tried this alternative decomposition approach, when we analyzed the inequality trends in BRIC countries.

Table 3.2 shows that "within inequality" is a small fraction of total inequality. In other words, the levels of inequality within each group are very low and it simply implies the WDR grouping by per capita income creates homogeneous groups of countries. Most of the inequality is between the groups. As the table shows, "within inequality" has no clear time trend, whereas "between inequality" has a rising trend along with the 94-country inequality index. In view of the fact that there is no world government implementing systematic income transfers from the poor to the more poor countries, this result is not at all surprising. This also prepares the ground for the concept of uniform income transfers that may take place within a country.

3.3.　Uniform Income Transfers

As mentioned earlier, income transfer is uniform if the transfer is from the above average to below average earners, the size of the transfer being proportional to the actual income earned and average income. We propose to demonstrate that if a policy of uniform income transfers is followed, then interpersonal, interregional, and intraregional income distributions change in the same direction. The policies that result in uniform redistribution of income without discriminating between regions or between groups within a region are the direct taxes, such as income, wealth, and property taxes. Redistribution through indirect taxes is not uniform, because these taxes are based on expenditure and therefore discriminate against an individual or a region having a lower-than-average income but a higher-than-average expenditure. The bias in income transfer brought about by the presence of indirect taxes is, however, partly offset by the fact that the inequality in consumption expenditure can be expected to be uniformly lower than the inequality in income, as the proportion of income saved rises with the size of income across income earners. While this may be a partial justification for restricting our analysis only to uniform transfers, there are other considerations that suggest that the income transfers actually taking place in a society are not uniform. A deviation from uniformity occurs when public spending does not discriminate between the rich and the poor. Because of the character of non-exclusivity of public goods, such nonuniformity cannot be avoided. However, progressive direct tax rates that prevail in almost all countries can be expected to correct some of this nonuniformity. On the whole, it may not be too unrealistic to base a conceptual framework to study income distribution on income transfers that are uniform. If income transfers are uniform, such transfers unfailingly improve income distribution irrespective of the size of the transfer. Uniform income transfers, taken as a benchmark, can be used to find out how far the actual transfers have deviated from uniformity, thus indicating the failure of the policy in reducing inequality and poverty in the country.

We have already discussed the meaning of uniform income transfer and the forces acting for and against uniformity in the redistribution of income. What remains to be established is the arithmetic of income transfers that cause unidirectional movements in the interpersonal, interstate, and intrastate income inequality. Such transfers can take place at various levels: interpersonal, interregional, and interclass. It is a simple arithmetic exercise to show that if the transfers that take place at the interpersonal level are uniform, then the transfers are also uniform at higher degree of aggregation, that is, at the interregional and interclass levels.

Let Y_{ijk} be the income earned by the ith person belonging to the jth income class and residing in the kth state and $\overline{Y}$ is the per capita income. Superscripts are used to date the variables. A uniform redistribution of incomes between time $t - 1$ and time t is defined as

$$Y_{ijk}^t = Y_{ijk}^{t-1} - \lambda(Y_{ijk}^{t-1} - \overline{Y}^{t-1}), \quad 0 < \lambda < 1. \tag{3.4}$$

Equation (3.4) shows that income is transferred from persons with more-than-average incomes to persons with less-than-average incomes. It shows that if a person's income is higher than average in time $t - 1$, then the person's income decreases between time $t - 1$ and t. It may be checked by aggregating Equation (3.4) with respect to all i, j, and k that $Y^t = Y^{t-1}$ with Y representing GNP, so that there is no income growth between the two periods. Also, an increase in λ makes income distribution more equal by raising the size of the transfer. The maximum value of λ is unity in which case everyone has the same income. Aggregating Equation (3.4) with respect to i and k and writing Y_j to represent the total income of the jth income class and n_j to represent the number of people in the jth income class, we get

$$Y_j^t = Y_j^{t-1} - \lambda(Y_j^{t-1} - n_j \overline{Y}^{t-1}).$$ (3.5)

Equation (3.5), written in terms of per capita incomes, is

$$\frac{Y_j^t}{n_j} = \frac{Y_j^{t-1}}{n_j} - \lambda \left(\frac{Y_j^{t-1}}{n_j} - \overline{Y}^{t-1} \right),$$ (3.5a)

which shows that an increase in λ improves income distribution by income class.

Now aggregating Equation (3.4) with respect to i and j and writing Y_k for the total income of the kth region and n_k for the number of people located in the kth region, we get the same result for interstate income distribution:

$$\frac{Y_k^t}{n_k} = \frac{Y_k^{t-1}}{n_k} - \lambda \left(\frac{Y_k^{t-1}}{n_k} - \overline{Y}^{t-1} \right).$$ (3.5b)

Since the basis of interstate transfer according to the uniformity rule is the difference between a state's per capita income (Y_k/n_k) and the country's per capita income $(\overline{Y})$, the Theil measure of interstate inequality defined in Equation (3.1) will capture the extent to which interstate transfers have deviated from the uniformity rule.

Finally, aggregating Equation (3.4) with respect to i and writing Y_{jk} to denote the aggregate income earned by all earners belonging to the jth income class and residing in the kth state and n_{jk} to denote the number of persons in the jth income class and residing in the kth state, we get the redistribution rules within each state:

$$\frac{Y_{jk}^t}{n_{jk}} = \frac{Y_{jk}^{t-1}}{n_{jk}} - \lambda \left(\frac{Y_{jk}^{t-1}}{n_{jk}} - \overline{Y} \right).$$ (3.5c)

An increase in λ, therefore, is seen to improve personal, class-wise, interstate and intrastate income distributions, provided that the income transfers are uniform.

The decomposition of the Theil measure to capture the effects of uniform income transfers on income distribution at different levels in a federal economy is what remains to be seen. We have shown that the Theil measure is decomposable and total inequality can be broken into components. If income transfers are uniform, then the trends in total inequality and the trends in the inequality in the components will be similar. However, one cannot expect the income transfers to be always uniform at every level. Theil index of inequality, therefore, would measure the extent to which income transfers have been uniform. There are studies on the effect of income transfers on inequality and growth that use Theil's index or Gini index. For instance, Keane and Prasad (2002) have shown, by using Gini coefficient, that social transfer mechanisms in Poland, including pensions, played an important role in mitigating increases in both overall inequality and poverty during 1990–1997.

If there is no growth component in the income generation process, uniform income transfer will achieve absolute equality in income distribution in the long run. To see this, we write Equation (3.4) separately for below average earners who receive transfers and above average earners who pay the tax. Let y_t and x_t be, respectively, the incomes of below and above average earners. Then,

$$y_t = y_{t-1} + \lambda(\overline{Y}_{t-1} - y_{t-1}), \quad \overline{Y}_{t-1} > y_{t-1}; \tag{3.4a}$$

$$x_t = x_{t-1} - \lambda(x_{t-1} - \overline{Y}_{t-1}), \quad \overline{Y}_{t-1} < x_{t-1}. \tag{3.4b}$$

The difference equations in Equation (3.4a) and (3.4b) can be solved subject to the assumption that the extent of deprivation of the below average earners, $\overline{Y}_{t-1} - y_{t-1}$, is a linear, monotonically decreasing function of y_{t-1} and the extent of affluence, $x_{t-1} - \overline{Y}_{t-1}$, is a linear, monotonically increasing function of x_{t-1}. In other words, $\overline{Y}_{t-1} - y_{t-1} = \alpha - \beta y_{t-1}$, and $x_{t-1} - \overline{Y}_{t-1} = -\gamma + \delta x_{t-1}$. It is necessary to sum these linear equations over the number of below and above average earners to find consistency, which requires the following: $0 < \alpha < \overline{Y}_{t-1}, 0 < \beta < 1, 0 < \delta < 1, 0 < \gamma < \overline{Y}_{t-1}$. Substituting these linear functions in Equation (3.4a) and (3.4b) and solving, we get $y_t = \frac{\alpha}{\beta} + (1 - \lambda\beta)^t (y_0 - \frac{\alpha}{\beta})$ and $x_t = \frac{\gamma}{\delta} + (1 - \lambda\delta)^t (x_0 - \frac{\gamma}{\delta})$, respectively. It would be reasonable to assume that $y_0 < \frac{\alpha}{\beta}$ and $x_0 > \frac{\gamma}{\delta}$. The solutions of the difference equations show that the asymptotic value of y_t is $\frac{\alpha}{\beta}$ and that of x_t is $\frac{\gamma}{\delta}$, the only difference being that y_t converges to $\frac{\alpha}{\beta}$ from below and x_t converges to $\frac{\gamma}{\delta}$ from above. The purpose of all this is to show that in a growth-less economy, uniform income transfers will eliminate income inequality in the long run.

3.4.   Growth and Distribution

No economy will resemble the growth-less structure described above nor is income transfer exactly uniform. But we retain the mechanism of uniform income transfer and introduce a growth element in the income generation process. The framework of analysis we propose to apply in this study is an extension of the model of uniform income transfers where GNP is assumed to remain fixed. We now assume that the people earning below average do not save and those earning incomes above average save a fixed portion of their net incomes and earn interest or profit on their savings. Steady-state equilibrium may be disturbed by the government's policy of income transfers from the above average to the below average earners. Given the fixed rate of savings, this redistribution of income will reduce total savings and investment. But redistribution may raise the rate of return on investment, which may make up for reduction in the level of investment. Technological progress is another reason why incomes may rise at both above average and below average levels. But the important question is whether this growth process combined with uniform income transfer will improve income distribution.

Equation (3.4) can be changed in the following manner:

$$Y_{ijk}^t = Y_{ijk}^{t-1} - \lambda \left(Y_{ijk}^{t-1} - \overline{Y}^{t-1} \right) + \mu \left[s \left\{ Y_{ijk}^{t-1} - \lambda \left(Y_{ijk}^{t-1} - \overline{Y}^{t-1} \right) \right\} \right], \quad (3.6)$$

where s is the rate of savings and,

$$\begin{aligned} \mu &> 0 \quad \text{if} \quad Y_{ijk}^{t-1} \geq \overline{Y}^{t-1} \\ &= 0 \quad \text{otherwise} \end{aligned} \quad (3.7)$$

μ is the rate of interest in equilibrium which may be positively related to the distribution parameter λ, as a policy-induced reduction of savings, in the absence of technical progress, may increase its rate of return.

As may be recalled, there was no provision for income growth in Equation (3.4). The simple transfer mechanism illustrated in Equation (3.4) has been modified in Equations (3.6) and (3.7) to include an income growth component for the above average earners who save a part of their income. It is simply assumed that a part of income minus transfer is saved by earners who earn more than the average income and earn a return on this saving in the next time period. It is assumed for the sake of simplicity that the below average earners do not save. An understanding of the growth process represented by Equations (3.6) and (3.7) will require a distinction to be made between the below average and the above average earners.

We propose to look at income dynamics of four categories of earners. Group I includes the poorest earners whose incomes are much below the national average and no part of these incomes is saved. Group II earners have more incomes than group one earners, but their incomes are still below the national average, but they save a part of their income. The first two groups include only the below average earners who receive transfer payments. Group III and group IV earners have more incomes than the national average and therefore they pay a tax. The only difference between the last two groups is that group three earners do not save, while group four earners save a part of the disposable income. The earners in the first and the third groups are comparable to the two groups of below and above average earners in the growth-less economy.

Let y_t, z_t, w_t, and x_t be the incomes of four classes of income earners, respectively, at time t. While λ is the transfer parameter and μ is the rate of return on income saved, we use two savings rates, s_1 and s_2 for the second and fourth categories of earners. The time paths of incomes for these four groups of earners are defined as follows:

Group I: The poorest among below average earners receiving transfers with no savings

$$y_t = y_{t-1} + \lambda \left(\overline{Y}_{t-1} - y_{t-1} \right), \quad \overline{Y}_{t-1} > y_{t-1}. \tag{3.8}$$

Group II: Below average earners receiving transfers and saving.

$$z_t = z_{t-1} + \lambda \left(\overline{Y}_{t-1} - z_{t-1} \right) + \mu\, s_1 \left[z_{t-1} + \lambda \left(\overline{Y}_{t-1} - z_{t-1} \right) \right],$$
$$\overline{Y}_{t-1} > z_{t-1}. \tag{3.9}$$

Group III: Above average earners paying tax but not saving.

$$w_t = w_{t-1} - \lambda \left(w_{t-1} - \overline{Y}_{t-1} \right), \quad \overline{Y}_{t-1} < w_{t-1}. \tag{3.10}$$

Group IV: Above average earners paying tax and saving.

$$x_t = x_{t-1} - \lambda \left(x_{t-1} - \overline{Y}_{t-1} \right) + \mu\, s_2 \left[x_{t-1} - \lambda \left(x_{t-1} - \overline{Y}_{t-1} \right) \right],$$
$$\overline{Y}_{t-1} < x_{t-1}. \tag{3.11}$$

The difference equations in Equations (3.8) through (3.11) can be solved subject to an assumption regarding the extent of deprivation of below average earners and the extent of affluence of the above average earners. Obviously, the former declines and the latter rises, with any increase in personal income. We hypothesize a linear relationship between deprivation or affluence and personal income:

$$\overline{Y}_{t-1} - y_{t-1} = a_0 - b\,y_{t-1}, \quad o < a_0 < \overline{Y}_{t-1}, \quad 0 < b < 1. \quad (3.12)$$

$$\overline{Y}_{t-1} - z_{t-1} = a_1 - b\,z_{t-1}, \quad 0 < a_1 < \overline{Y}_{t-1}. \quad (3.13)$$

Since $z_{t-1} > y_{t-1}$ for all t, it follows that $a_0 > a_1$.

$$w_{t-1} - \overline{Y}_{t-1} = -k + d\,w_{t-1}, \quad 0 < k < \overline{Y}_{t-1}, \quad 0 < d < 1. \quad (3.14)$$

$$x_{t-1} - \overline{Y}_{t-1} = c + d\,x_{t-1}, \quad 0 < c < \overline{Y}_{t-1}, \quad 0 < d < 1. \quad (3.15)$$

Since $x_{t-1} > w_{t-1}$ for all t, it also implies that $d < 1$.

The solutions of the difference equations in Equations (3.8) through (3.11) subject to the assumptions in Equations (3.12) through (3.15) are as follows:

$$y_t = y_e + (y_0 - y_e)(1 - \lambda b)^t$$
$$y_e \equiv a_0/b \quad (3.16)$$

$$z_t = \frac{f_0}{1 - g_0} + \left[z_0 - \frac{f_0}{1 - g_0} \right] g_0^t, \quad f_0 \equiv \lambda a_1(1 + \mu s_1),$$
$$g_0 \equiv (1 + \mu s_1)(1 - \lambda b). \quad (3.17)$$

$$w_t = \frac{k}{d} + \left(w_0 - \frac{k}{d} \right)(1 - \lambda d)^t. \quad (3.18)$$

$$x_t = \frac{f_1}{(g_1 - 1)} + \left[x_0 - \frac{f_1}{(g_1 - 1)} \right] g_1^t$$
$$g_1 \equiv (1 + \mu s_2)(1 - \lambda d)$$
$$f_1 \equiv \lambda c(1 + \mu s_2) \quad (3.19)$$

We assume that for the first group of below average earners $y_0 < y_e$ in Equation (3.16). An increase in transfer intensity, represented by λ, raises every earner's income in this group. Since $(1 - \lambda b) < 1$, incomes converge to y_e. Incomes in the second group grow due to two reasons: transfer and returns earned on savings. We assume that $z_0 > f_0/(1 - g_0)$ to make sure that incomes do not decline over time in this group. If the savings rate, s_1, is low, which is likely to be the case in this group and if the transfer intensity, λ, is sufficiently high, then $g_0 < 1$. Under these conditions the incomes in the second group converge to $f_0/(1 - g_0)$. Incomes in the third group are higher than the national average and, therefore, subject to taxes, but there is no saving. Since $(1 - \lambda d) < 1$, incomes converge to $\frac{k}{d}$. For the above average earners in the fourth group, unless a drastic redistribution is taking place with λ taking high values and s_1 taking very low values, which is unlikely in this group, g_1 is likely to be greater than one.[1] With the assumption that $x_0 > f_1/(g_1 - 1)$, incomes in this group are likely to diverge.

The annual growth rates of personal incomes,[2] G_t^{bI}, G_t^{bII} in the below average groups and G_t^{aIII}, G_t^{aIV} in the above average categories can be calculated from Equations (3.16) to (3.19), which also brings us to the propositions relating to income convergence.

$$G_t^{bI} = \frac{\lambda \, b(y_e - y_0)}{y_0 + y_e \left[(1 - \lambda b)^{1-t} - 1\right]}. \tag{3.20}$$

$$G_t^{bII} = \frac{\left(z_0 - \frac{f_0}{1-g_0}\right)(g_0 - 1)}{z_0 + \frac{f_0\left(g_0^{1-t}-1\right)}{(1-g_0)}}. \tag{3.21}$$

$$G_t^{aIII} = \frac{-\lambda d\left(w_0 - \frac{k}{d}\right)}{w_0 + \frac{k}{d}\left\{(1 - \lambda d)^{1-t} - 1\right\}}. \tag{3.22}$$

$$G_t^{aIV} = \frac{\left(x_0 - \frac{f_1}{g_1-1}\right)(g_1 - 1)}{x_0 + \frac{f_1\left(g_1^{1-t}-1\right)}{(g_1-1)}}. \tag{3.23}$$

---

[1] The precise condition for g to be greater than one is: $\mu s_1 > \lambda d/(1 - \lambda d)$ which is satisfied if either μ is high or λ is low.

[2] Growth rates are defined as the difference of incomes at t and $t - 1$ divided by income at $t - 1$. With $g_1 > 1$, G_t^{aIV} tends to $g_1 - 1$, as t tends to infinity. The asymptotic growth rates of the first three groups tend to zero, as $g_0, (1 - \lambda b)$ and $(1 - \lambda d)$ are less than unity.

Proposition I

Incomes of below average earners and non-saving above average earners converge and those of above average earners who save diverge in the sense that the relatively more affluent among the below average earners become less affluent over time and the relatively more affluent among the above average earners become more affluent over time. Thus, if the initial income distribution is unequal with the number of below average earners far exceeding the number of above average earners, who save a part of their incomes, growth will cause greater equality in income distribution.

It is obvious from Equations (3.20) and (3.21) that $\partial G_t^{bI}/\partial\, y_0 < 0$ and $\partial G_t^{bII}/\partial z_0 < 0$. It is also easy to show from Equations (3.22) and (3.23) that $\partial G_t^{aIII}/\partial w_0 < 0$ and $\partial G_t^{aIV}/\partial\, x_0 > 0$. In other words, lower the initial level of personal income of a below average earner or an above average non-saving earner, higher is the rate at which income grows over time causing convergence of income. The opposite is true for above average earners.

There is nothing in the growth process that prevents income distribution to turn more equal, while the economy is on a high growth path. An increased intensity of transfer (higher value of λ) does not necessarily raise the growth rates of incomes of below average earners just as it does not necessarily reduce the growth rates of incomes of above average earners. It can be easily ascertained that the derivatives of all four growth rates with respect to λ have indeterminate signs. The reason is quite simple. If the intensity of transfer is raised, a below average earner will get higher income at t that may take the earner closer to the average earner. Thus, in $t + 1$, less income will be transferred causing a reduction in the income growth rate of the below average earner. The process operates in the opposite direction for above average earners whose incomes may grow at higher rates at $t + 1$ when they pay lower tax, having made a transfer at t. The following proposition summarizes the arguments:

Proposition II

The effect of the intensity of transfers on growth rates of incomes in both the above average and below average categories is indeterminate. In other words, there is no systematic effect of the uniform income transfers on the growth process.

Now we look at the process of accumulation represented by two parameters, the savings rate (s) and the rate of return (μ). The expressions for g and f, figuring in G_t^{bII} and G_t^{aIV} defined in Equations (3.21) and (3.23) depend on both accumulation and redistribution. There is no direct relationship between G_t^{bI} or G_t^{aIII} and the accumulation parameters, because the income growth among these non-saving earners depends only on redistribution. But growth is sure to raise average income which means accumulation does indirectly affect the income growth rates of the below average earners and causes more transfers from above average to below average earners. Whether this has an adverse effect on the process of accumulation is difficult to say. The effect of a change in accumulation parameters, s or μ, on the growth rates of incomes in the above average category is indeterminate. An increase in the savings rate or rate of return will surely raise the incomes of the above average earners but they also pay more in taxes. They do experience a net increase in incomes but it is difficult to say if their income growth rates will increase as a result of higher savings rate or rate of return on savings. This indeterminacy is reinforced by the fact that the rate of return on savings may be partly determined by the transfer intensity. Thus, theoretically it is possible to have higher growth rates of income along with greater equality in the distribution of income.

Proposition III

The effect of higher savings rate or higher return on investment on the rates of growth of incomes is indeterminate among the above average earners. But insofar as accumulation raises average income, greater transfer raises the growth rates of incomes among the below average earners, as $\partial G_t^{bl}/\partial y_e > 0$.

In view of the propositions stated above what clearly appears is that high growth rate may result from the process of accumulation and that the growth process may lead to higher equality in the distribution of incomes provided that the initial level of income distribution is characterized by high degrees of inequality. Whether this theory is valid is an empirical question. The framework presented here does not establish an exact relationship between economic growth and income inequality. What the model suggests is that the initial conditions are important in the relationship between inequality and economic growth. There are several assumptions that are not quite realistic, such as a single transfer parameter applied to all groups. Moreover, the actual income transfers do not follow the mechanism of uniform income transfers, which is just a convenient assumption. Our purpose has been to identify the factors that may play a crucial role in the dynamics of growth and distribution. In a growth-less economy, uniform income transfers eliminate income disparities over time. Income growth, driven by accumulation or technological progress, is likely to be associated with increases in income inequality. But there is no exact relationship between economic growth and income distribution. Growth may also reduce income inequality. In any empirical study, it would not be surprising to find a positive relationship between growth and inequality. For instance, in a panel regression Forbes (2000) has found a significant positive relationship between inequality and growth, indicating that a country has to position itself in a growth–inequality trade-off growth, where growth rate is taken as a function of inequality measure of the previous year, income, male and female human capital, market distortions, and country and period dummy variables for a sample of 45 countries for the time period between 1966 and 1995. However, such intercountry studies on growth–inequality relationship are likely to be misleading due to two reasons. First, each country is unique in terms of its policies and institutions and second, a sample classification based on initial conditions is likely to generate more reliable results.

A decomposition of Gini index, defined in Equation (3.3), along the lines of this model can produce a relationship between growth on the one hand and inequality and poverty on the other, as Gini index can be separately computed for below average and above average earners for every year and these can be related to the overall index.[3]

$$G + \frac{n+1}{n} = G_B \, \rho_B \, \frac{\bar{y}_B}{\bar{Y}} + G_A \, \rho_A \, \frac{\bar{x}_A}{\bar{Y}}. \qquad (3.24)$$

---

[3] The decomposition of Gini coefficient is done for only two groups of earners, below and above average, using the solutions in Equation (16).

$G_B \equiv \frac{2\sum_{i=1}^{n_B} iy_i}{n_B \sum_{i=1}^{n_B} y_i} - \frac{n_B+1}{n_B}$ is the Gini measure of inequality among below aver-

age earners whose number is n_B. $G_A \equiv \frac{2\sum_{j=1}^{n_A} jx_j}{n_A \sum_{j=1}^{n_A} x_j} - \frac{n_A+1}{n_A}$ is the Gini measure

of inequality among the above average earners whose number is n_B, $n_A +$
$n_B = n$. $\bar{y}_B = \frac{1}{n_B}\sum_{i=1}^{n_B} y_i$ *and* $\bar{x}_A = \frac{1}{n_A}\sum_{j=1}^{n_A} x_j$ are, respectively, the average
incomes of the below and above average earners, whereas $\overline{Y} = \frac{1}{n}\sum_{i=1}^{n} Y_i$ is
the average income for all groups of earners. Therefore, $\frac{\bar{y}_B}{\overline{Y}}$ *and* $\frac{\bar{x}_A}{\overline{Y}}$ are,
respectively, the average income shares of the below and above aver-
age earners. $\rho_B \equiv \frac{n_B(n_B+1)}{n^2}$ *and* $\rho_A \equiv \frac{n_A(n_A+1)}{n^2}$ are related to the population shares of the below and above average income earners but they
are not exactly the same as population shares. $\rho_B \geq \rho_A$, *if* $n_B \geq n_A$ *and*
$\rho_B < \rho_A$ *if* $n_B < n_A$. $\rho_B + \rho_A \neq 1$. Every term in Equation (3.16) has
variations over time. For a fixed population, only one term, that is, n is
fixed. The overall inequality depends on inequality among below average earners (G_B), inequality among above average earners (G_A), average
income shares of below and above average earners, and the parameters
ρ_B *and* ρ_A, which are somewhat related to the population proportions of
these two groups of earners. The theory of growth and distribution suggests
that G_B declines over time and G_A rises at a decreasing rate. Aggregation
of Equation (3.16) for incomes of all below average earners yields the fol-
lowing: $\bar{y}_B = y_e + (\bar{y}_{B0} - y_e)(1 - \lambda b)^t$, where $\bar{y}_B$ is the average income
of the below average earners and $\bar{y}_{B0}$ is the base year average. $\bar{y}_B$ increases
over time and converges to y_e, if $\bar{y}_{B0} < y_e$. This would be the case if the
level of poverty in the base year is high. With only two groups of income
earners, the average income shares of below and above average earners are
inversely related as

$$\frac{\bar{x}_A}{\overline{Y}} = \frac{n}{n_A} - \frac{n_B}{n_A}\frac{\bar{y}_B}{\overline{Y}}. \qquad (3.25)$$

Using Equation (3.25) in Equation (3.24), we get the following relationship
between overall income inequality and inequality levels among the below
and above average earners.

$$G + \frac{n+1}{n} = \left[G_B\rho_B - \frac{n_B}{n_A}G_A\rho_A\right]\frac{\overline{Y}_B}{\overline{Y}} + \frac{n}{n_A}G_A\rho_A. \qquad (3.26)$$

In Equation (3.26), we take $(n+1)/n$ to be equal to unity. Overall income inequality, measured by G depends on inequality levels among the below average earners (G_B), inequality levels among above average earners (G_A), their respective population shares and numbers. G also depends on average incomes of these two groups of earners and the country's per capital income, $\overline{Y}$. Even though there are too many factors in play, one may roughly predict what would happen to the overall income inequality in a country's high growth phase in which the rate of growth of per capita income is very high. The first term on the right-hand side of Equation (3.26) is positive, if income inequality among the below average earner is high and the income inequality among the above average earners is sufficiently low. Under these conditions, a high rate of growth of $\overline{Y}$ would reduce the average income share of the below average earners, compensating for rising $\overline{Y}_B$ in the process of growth and redistribution during which n_A rises relative to n, as some of the below average earners move up to the category of above average earners. Proposition IV summarizes this argument.

Proposition IV

If the levels of income inequality and poverty among the below average earners are sufficiently high and income inequality among the above average earners is sufficiently low, a high rate of growth of per capita income is likely to reduce overall income inequality.

The models presented in this chapter depict the complexity in the relationship between economic growth and income inequality. One simplifying assumption made in these models, namely the uniform income transfer, will probably not hold in the real world, but it enables us to understand the complexities of the process of economic growth. The growth experiences of BRIC are extremely diverse and it may be unrealistic to expect some kind of uniformity in their growth and inequality patterns. In Chapter 5, the patterns of regional inequality in these four countries over long periods of time are discussed, dividing the periods into sub-periods to capture regime changes. The econometric framework is the random coefficient model to find out whether income convergence is taking place among the below average regions and whether income divergence is the story for the above average regions. The results are not always consistent with the model of this chapter and one possible explanation is the failure of social transfer mechanism. The story is unique as well as interesting for each country, though there is some commonality that is observed. We have also sorted the data to capture the effects of (i) high or low inequality regimes, (ii) high or low growth regimes, (iii) high or low corruption regimes, and (iv) high or low government spending, on the patterns of growth and inequality in BRIC.

CHAPTER 4

Descriptive Statistics and Basic Regression Estimates for BRIC

4.1. India

The NAS published by Central Statistical Organization (CSO) is the source of data on regional economic activities in India, such as net domestic product (NDP) and its sector-wise breakdown at the national as well as state level. The estimates are available at constant prices, but frequent changes in the base year make it difficult to compile a continuous time series for a long time period. Trend growth rates are reported in Table 4.1 for three periods that somewhat overlap. The post-reform period, 1999–2008, shows the highest rate of growth of per capita net domestic product (NDP), NDP and infrastructure, while the growth rates of manufacturing, services, and agriculture have been the highest in the first period. Earlier estimates of growth rates reported in Das and Barua (1996) during 1982–1992 at 1970–1971 prices show much lower growth rates for agriculture, manufacturing, and services. All trend growth rates are statistically significant, and even a casual comparison with the Das–Barua estimates clearly establishes the fact that economic reforms introduced in 1991 have accelerated the pace of economic growth in all sectors of the Indian economy, except perhaps in agriculture. This is not really surprising as the period 1967–1978 is regarded as the period of Green Revolution in India during which major changes in farming technology, such as introduction of high-yield variety of seed, improved land productivity substantially.

Das and Barua (1996) report rising trends in the interstate income inequality in almost all sectors during 1970–1992. This observation is still valid, as the following tables and graphs would show, the only difference being that in the post-reform phase, the Indian economy has grown much faster and does not have to take the worst of both worlds, that is, economic growth and income distribution. We have used the Theil's entropy

Table 4.1.   Annual average growth rates (%) by sectors (industry of origin).[a]

	1980–1997 (at 1980–1981 prices)	1993–2001 (at 1993–1994 prices)	1999–2008 (at 1999–2000 prices)	1982–1992 (at 1970–1971 prices)[b]
Agriculture	4.15	2.38	2.82	3.2
Agriculture and primary	3.92	2.66	3.14	3.4[c]
Manufacturing	10.72	4.95	6.87	6.5
Infrastructure	8.83	11.18	14.92	6.5
Services	10.12	8.75	8.03	6.2
NDP	7.46	5.64	7.49	5.1
Population	2.19	1.78	1.53	2.06
Per capita NDP	3.24	3.97	5.58	3.2

Note: [a]Infrastructure includes electricity, gas and water supply plus transport, storage, communication, and construction. (For infrastructure, the state of A&N Islands has been removed from the dataset because all data are negative for most years.) Primary includes forestry and logging, fishing, and mining and quarrying. Services include trade, hotels and restaurants plus banking and insurance plus real estate, ownership of dwellings and business services plus public administration and other services. All income categories are the same as defined by CSO.
[b]Estimates from Das and Barua (1996), Table 7.
[c]Growth rate of primary only.
Source: CSO, Directorates of Economics & Statistics of respective State Governments (Ministry of Statistics and Programme Implementation).

measure defined in Equation (3.1) in Chapter 3. The values are multiplied by 100 for visual convenience. Table 4.2 has these estimates for the period 1980–1981 to 1996–1997. The graph drawn in Figure 4.1 shows rising trends, particularly after 1991. Very sharp increases in interstate inequality in manufacturing output need special mention.

Table 4.3 and Figure 4.2 have the entropy estimates for the period 1993–1994 to 2000–2001. Apart from the volatility in primary sector inequality, the story is basically the same, that is, rising inequality in the interstate distribution of economic activities. The story is somewhat different in the last period, that is, 1999–2000 to 2007–2008. Table 4.4 and Figure 4.3 seem to suggest that even though the levels of inequality have

Table 4.2. Entropy estimates at constant prices for 25 states and union territories (at 1980–1981 prices).

	Primary	Agriculture and primary	Manufacturing	Infrastructure	Services	NSDP
1980–1981	3.92	3.38	21.66	10.49	9.65	4.73
1981–1982	4.61	3.75	18.90	11.01	9.49	4.70
1982–1983	5.29	4.40	17.90	11.76	9.92	4.97
1983–1984	4.25	3.66	18.05	12.00	9.57	4.61
1984–1985	4.00	3.32	17.18	12.23	9.11	4.71
1985–1986	4.63	3.99	19.18	12.17	10.15	5.25
1986–1987	4.67	3.95	20.60	11.52	9.87	5.21
1987–1988	5.74	4.80	17.32	11.98	9.52	5.53
1988–1989	5.27	4.33	16.94	11.61	9.38	5.31
1989–1990	5.59	4.61	17.55	12.91	9.74	6.29
1990–1991	5.39	4.35	18.81	12.70	9.60	5.98
1991–1992	6.33	4.91	18.51	13.11	11.38	6.57
1992–1993	6.61	5.32	22.29	14.11	12.02	7.98
1993–1994	6.58	5.31	23.65	15.66	13.32	8.52
1994–1995	6.44	5.35	25.98	15.31	13.74	8.95
1995–1996	7.06	5.86	26.70	15.81	14.71	9.73
1996–1997	7.87	6.49	26.52	16.19	14.24	9.74

Note: NSDP: Net State Domestic Product.
Source: CSO, Directorates of Economics & Statistics of respective State Governments (Ministry of Statistics and Programme Implementation).

reached high figures, some degree of stability have been observed in all sectors except in manufacturing and primary.

As mentioned in Chapter 3, Theil decomposition shown in Equation (3.2) can be done in an alternative way to estimate the average contributions of sectors of the economy toward the overall regional income inequality. Table 4.5 has the estimates of a regression of Net State Domestic Product (NSDP) entropy values on the entropies of manufacturing, infrastructure, service, and combined agriculture and primary, in the double-log format subject to the restriction that the coefficients add to unity. The coefficients are estimates of percentage change in NSDP entropy for every 1%

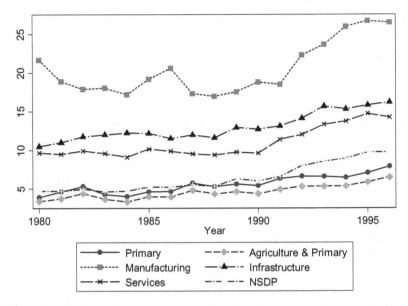

Figure 4.1.   Time trend of entropy estimates by sectors from 1980 to 1997.

Table 4.3.   Entropy estimates at constant prices for 31 states and union territories (at 1993–1994 prices).[a]

Year	NSDP	Agri-culture	Primary	Agriculture and primary	Manufac-turing	Service	Infra-structure
1993–1994	7.08	5.39	25.91	4.34	23.96	11.01	12.56
1994–1995	7.11	5.62	27.93	4.69	23.26	11.20	13.63
1995–1996	8.06	6.34	26.95	5.39	25.12	12.38	14.36
1996–1997	7.88	6.93	27.57	5.88	25.28	12.14	15.04
1997–1998	8.46	7.22	30.17	6.43	25.75	13.10	16.36
1998–1999	8.74	7.22	25.99	6.36	28.92	13.44	16.16
1999–2000	8.82	8.07	22.23	7.03	27.40	14.27	15.24
2000–2001	8.84	9.46	25.95	7.53	27.26	14.28	16.94

Note: [a]Mizoram has been removed from the dataset due to limited data availability.
Source: CSO, Directorates of Economics & Statistics of respective State Governments (Ministry of Statistics and Programme Implementation).

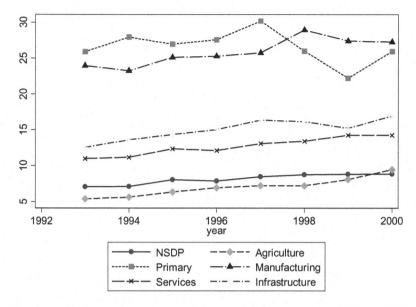

Figure 4.2. Time trend of entropy estimates by sectors from 1993 to 2001.

Table 4.4. Entropy estimates at constant prices for 31 states and union territories (at 1999–2000 prices).

Year	NSDP	Agri-culture	Primary	Agriculture and primary	Manufac-turing	Service	Infra-structure
1999–2000	7.45	6.77	19.06	5.53	22.32	12.14	9.80
2000–2001	7.42	6.98	19.51	5.49	22.11	11.76	10.26
2001–2002	7.66	6.51	19.57	5.69	22.11	12.10	10.23
2002–2003	8.17	7.03	19.86	5.57	22.70	12.89	10.75
2003–2004	8.37	7.75	20.98	6.69	24.21	13.01	11.40
2004–2005	8.62	6.82	22.46	5.87	24.13	13.75	11.64
2005–2006	9.48	7.39	21.73	6.52	26.38	15.21	10.74
2006–2007	9.60	6.59	23.95	5.91	27.10	15.90	10.45
2007–2008	9.98	7.81	25.19	7.06	27.34	16.10	10.65

Source: CSO, Directorates of Economics & Statistics of respective State Governments (Ministry of Statistics and Programme Implementation).

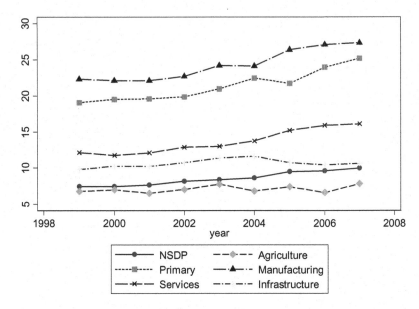

Figure 4.3. Time trend of entropy estimates by sectors from 1999 to 2007.

change in a sector's entropy. This is not an explanatory regression and its purpose is to find the relative contribution of sectors to the overall inequality. Interstate inequality in service has the biggest positive contribution to overall inequality in all three periods. Manufacturing and infrastructure have negative contributions in the first period. In the second period, manufacturing and agriculture contribute negatively. In the last period, except for manufacturing, which has a negative contribution, all sectors positively contribute to the overall inequality.

Table 4.6 has the estimates of the correlation coefficients between annual growth rates and entropy measures of inequality. The results are quite different from the estimates of Das and Barua (1996), where most coefficients were negative during the period 1971–1992, which was a phase of low growth rates in the Indian economy. In the first and the third periods, our estimates show positive correlation, and negative correlation is shown only in the middle period. There is plenty of evidence to suggest that regional inequalities have contributed growth or growth has contributed to greater regional inequality in India during the high growth phase. As regard personal income inequality, the OECD study by Arnal

Table 4.5.   Regression results.

	Time period: 1980–1997 dependent variable: ln (entropy of NSDP)	Time period: 1993–2001 dependent variable: ln (entropy of NSDP)	Time period: 1999–2008 dependent variable: ln (entropy of NSDP)
ln (entropy of manufacturing)	−0.22 (−0.62)	−0.89[c] (−1.82)	−0.47[a] (−5.98)
ln (entropy of infrastructure)	−0.37 (−0.95)	0.26 (0.52)	0.14[c] (1.8)
ln (entropy of service)	1.19[c] (1.71)	1.81[a] (2.45)	1.12[a] (10.54)
ln (entropy of agriculture and primary)	0.39 (1.57)	−0.19 (−0.49)	0.19[a] (2.65)
REPS	500	500	500
Root-mean-square error	0.11	0.05	0.008

Note: Figures in the parenthesis are *z* scores. Standard errors are obtained through bootstrapping.
Seed = 10,101; REPS = Number of repetitions.
All 1980–1997 data are in 1980–1981 prices; 1993–2005 data are in 1993–1994 prices, and 1999–2008 data are in 1999–2000 prices;
[a]indicates significance at 1% level of significance;
[b]indicates significance at 5% level of significance;
[c]indicates significance at 10% level of significance.

and Förster (2010) shows an increase in income inequality, measured by Gini coefficient of household incomes, between 1990s and 2000s, indicating unidirectional movements of regional inequality and personal income inequality. A study by Nayyar (2008) shows that during 1978–1979 to 2002–2003, 16 Indian states were not converging to identical levels of per capita incomes in the steady state and there was evidence that the states were converging to increasingly divergent steady states, indicative of rising interstate disparities in the levels of private and public investment and an insignificant equalizing impact of transfers from the federal to the state governments. Our estimates, along with the studies cited here, indicate

Table 4.6. Correlation coefficient between entropy measures of inequality and the corresponding annual growth rates.

Category	1981–1997	1993–2001	1999–2008
Manufacturing	0.14[b]	−0.58[a]	0.25[c]
Services	0.26[a]	−0.21[c]	0.31[a]
Agriculture and primary	0.33[a]	−0.22[c]	0.29[c]
Infrastructure	0.28[a]	−0.44[a]	0.13

Note: [a]Indicates significance at 1% level of significance; [b]indicates significance at 5% level of significance; [c]indicates significance at 10% level of significance.

the failure of income transfer mechanism in the Indian economy. However, growth has probably contributed to poverty reduction. Ghosh (2010) has made estimates of rural and urban poverty and claims that during the period of 1987–1988 to 2004–2005, both urban and rural poverty have declined and that urban poverty has decreased faster than rural poverty.

4.2. China

The *Statistical Yearbooks* published annually by China National Bureau of Statistics are the primary sources of information on economic activities at the sectoral as well as provincial levels. During the Mao Zedong era (1949–1976), data are available for only three sectors: primary, secondary, and tertiary only at current prices. The sum of value added in these sectors is GRP. The sectors in the post-Mao era are primary, industry, infrastructure, and services, and value added figures can be computed at constant prices. Table 4.7 has the trend growth rates for three periods: 1952–1977 for the Mao Zedong era, 1978–1984 which is the post-Cultural Revolution period when four modernization programs for agriculture, industry, national defense, and science and technology were launched, and the modern period, 1984–2010. Policy mistakes, natural disasters, and extreme food shortages are reflected in a very low growth rate of primary sector at even current prices during the Mao era which was the revolutionary period known for class conflict. High growth rates in secondary and tertiary sectors as well as GRP growth rate during this period are probably illusory,

Table 4.7. Annual average growth rates (%) by sectors (industry of origin).[a]

	1952–1977 (at 1952 prices)	1952–1977 (at current prices)[b]		1978–1984 (at 1978 prices)	1984–2010 (at 1984 prices)
Primary		6.67	Primary	3.96	17.05
Secondary		37.35	Industry	−1.89	5.57
Tertiary		12.43	Infrastructure	−0.52	3.32
			Services	0.75	14.96
GRP	0.97	14.98	GRP[c]	0.11	9.93
Population	2.6	2.6	Population	0.61	1.07
Per capita GRP	−0.96	7.97	Per capita GRP	−0.47	6.23

Note: [a]*Infrastructure* includes transportation, storage, postal and telecommunications, and construction. *Primary* refers to agriculture (including farming, forestry, animal husbandry, and fishery). *Industry* includes mining and quarrying, manufacturing, production and supply of electricity, water and gas. *Services* include wholesale, retail and catering trade; banking, insurance, geological survey, water conservancy management, real estates, service for residents, service for agriculture, forestry, animal husbandry, fishery, subsidiary services for transportation and communications, comprehensive technical services; services for education, culture and arts, broadcasting, movies, television, public health, sports, social welfare, and scientific research; government agencies, political parties, social organizations, and military and police service. [b]The data during 1952–1977 are in current prices. Price index data for this period are not available for all sectors. Thus, we present entropy estimates using current data. *Primary* industry includes agriculture, farming, forestry, animal husbandry, and fishery. *Secondary* industry includes mining and quarrying, manufacturing, production and supply of electricity, water and gas, and construction. *Tertiary* industry implies all other industries not included in primary or secondary industry. [c]All GRP data are real values. Real GRP in year X is derived proportionally from the index of real GRP in year X.

Source: China National Bureau of Statistics, *Statistical Yearbooks* (published annually).

because there is no way of knowing how these growth rates would look like in real terms. Sector-wise price indices are not available for the Mao era, but deflators for nominal GRP are available with 1952 as the base year. Real GRP growth rate has been only 0.97% compared to the nominal growth rate of 14.98% during 1952–1977, as a result of which growth rate of per capita real GRP has been negative. Very high population growth rate during this period is due to wide gaps between birth rates and death rates during 1950–1975 in China's demographic transition, as noted by Yabuki and Harner (1999). It should, however, be mentioned that Fan and Chan-Kang (2005) have used 2002 as the base year and estimated the GDP growth rate of 5.43% for the period 1952–1977. But there is no controversy regarding the fact that during the early 1960s, the Great Leap Forward began to produce difficulties in agriculture and industry. China was forced to import grain for the first time since the earlier land reforms in the 1950s. Much of the problem was caused by high production targets, which were not accompanied by a sufficient amount of capital and public investment in modern inputs, such as fertilizers or improved transportation networks. Economically, the Great Leap Forward was an unmitigated failure. As mentioned by Danner (2006), the agricultural sector became severely depressed. In 1959 and 1960, the gross value of agricultural output fell by 14% and 13%, respectively, causing widespread famine, especially in rural areas. Furthermore, in the years 1960–1962, industrial output plummeted due to the agricultural crisis, poor economic planning, and the withdrawal of Soviet assistance. The failure of the Great Leap Forward led to the retreat of Maoist policy. The radical leftist policies associated with Mao (and those who followed his revolutionary ideology) did not reappear until the Cultural Revolution. Recovery would be fueled by those who favored a less radical approach to economic development reform.

Dismal performance in the second period is the result of regime change and policy experimentation but it does indicate recovery of primary sector. Again, with a different choice of base year, the growth rate estimate for this period would be higher than what is reported here, as in Yueh (2010), where year-to-year real GDP growth rates decline in 1978–1981 and increase in 1981–1984, whereas we have reported the trend growth rate for the entire period. The last period is the high growth phase of modern China, with the service sector emerging as a dynamic sector. Even with a higher population growth rate relative to the second period, the rate of growth of per capita real GRP in the modern period looks very impressive. The success story of China, particularly after the mid-1990s, has been the subject of intense research as well as policy debates. According to Flaasbeck *et al.* (2005), the main elements in China's growth strategy after the mid-1990s are exchange rate policy, introduction of a wage-setting regime, macroeconomic demand management that was able to strike a balance between the challenges of globalization, and the need to modernize the domestic economy. Another view is due to Danner (2006), who stressed the crucial role of Deng Xiaoping's leadership that initiated a new era in China. Though Deng recognized, as did Mao, the basic conflict between economic development and social equality, Deng pushed to accelerate modernization and economic development. He sought to repair the damaging effects of the Maoist period by systematically dismantling most of Mao's policies. Policies implemented after 1978 shifted away from the emphasis on revolutionary struggle and ideological transformation that had characterized much of the years of the Maoist era. In fact, the reforms after 1978 stressed political stability and economic development through the pragmatic adoption of policies to solve pressing concrete issues facing China's modernization process. Deng Xiaoping's reforms were primarily concerned with improving productivity and efficiency by reducing bureaucratic centralization and making greater use of market mechanisms. Deng introduced a hybrid of Communism and Capitalism into China known as the "socialist market economy". He developed a program of gradual, but fundamental, reform of the economic system. Underlying the reform was a principle of gradualism; new measures were first to be locally implemented, and, if proven successful, nationally disseminated.

Provincial inequality in modern China has been measured by Theil's entropy index and these are reported in Table 4.8 and plotted in Figure 4.4. The estimates show high levels of provincial inequality in industry and service sectors and low levels of inequality in the primary sector. However, although regional inequality in primary and service sectors has grown during this period, inequality in industry has a declining trend. Regional inequality in infrastructure has declined from 2004. Overall inequality in GRP shows fluctuations, ending in a declining trend from 2004. Jian *et al.* (1996) have observed income convergence among provinces of China during 1978–1993 and our entropy estimates for the modern period only partly support this observation, as we find fluctuations in entropy estimates of regional inequality. Arnal and Förster (2010) have reported substantial decline in poverty in China, measured by headcount ratios during 1993–2008, but an increase in the Gini measure of household income

Table 4.8. Entropy estimates for 30 provinces during 1984–2010 (at 1984 prices).[a]

	Primary	Industry	Infrastructure	Services	GRP
1984	1.86	26.22	14.10	15.90	10.52
1985	1.81	25.87	13.96	18.25	10.46
1986	1.96	25.38	14.68	17.64	10.15
1987	1.97	24.48	15.06	17.82	9.67
1988	2.30	24.05	14.79	17.01	8.95
1989	2.13	23.66	15.68	16.39	8.64
1990	1.92	24.43	16.70	21.33	8.49
1991	2.02	23.84	16.65	21.38	8.89
1992	1.96	24.80	17.72	21.35	9.37
1993	2.35	25.22	17.73	23.09	9.88
1994	2.78	24.72	18.97	24.02	9.65
1995	2.53	24.29	17.83	21.64	9.06
1996	2.87	24.83	18.09	22.24	9.47
1997	2.73	25.23	18.34	21.71	9.78
1998	2.71	25.03	18.50	21.97	10.06
1999	2.67	25.25	18.89	22.21	10.35
2000	2.67	25.54	18.84	22.03	10.54
2001	2.88	24.27	18.80	21.98	10.39
2002	2.90	23.84	18.82	22.21	10.43
2003	2.99	23.85	18.93	21.45	10.33
2004	3.04	22.90	18.51	20.05	9.77
2005	2.75	21.78	18.36	20.08	9.30
2006	2.81	20.62	17.42	20.37	8.82
2007	3.15	19.43	16.54	20.67	8.24
2008	3.37	18.64	15.95	20.18	7.65
2009	3.49	17.39	15.60	20.38	7.43
2010	3.64	16.74	15.74	20.34	6.90

Note: [a]The province of Hainan (1984–2010) does not have any available data and is hence removed from the dataset.
Source: China National Bureau of Statistics, *Statistical Yearbooks* (published annually).

inequality between 1990s and 2000s (latest years available) in a point-to-point comparison. Ghosh (2010) has also observed substantial increases in inequality in household consumption, measured by Gini coefficients, both at the national as well as urban and rural levels during 1978–2002.

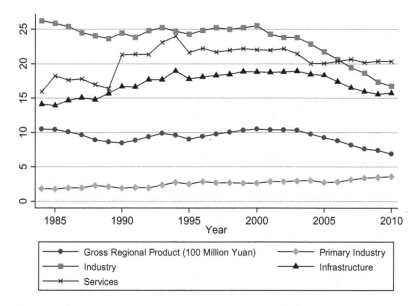

Figure 4.4. Time trend of entropy estimates by sectors from 1984 to 2010.

Inequality estimates for the middle period are shown in Table 4.8A and graphed in Figure 4.5. The pattern is very similar to that of the modern period, with insignificant levels of regional inequality in primary and high levels of inequality in industry and service sectors. The table also shows declining inequality trends in industry and service sectors and fluctuations in infrastructure inequality. This is also the period when the GRP growth rates have year-to-year fluctuations, as mentioned by Yueh (2010), which is reflected in the instability in the entropy measure of regional inequality in GRP.

Table 4.8B and Figure 4.6 have the entropy estimates of regional inequality during the Mao era, and here the story is completely different. The graphs show tremendous fluctuations in regional inequality in GRP, primary, secondary, and tertiary sectors. Regional inequality levels are very high in secondary and tertiary sectors. Primary sector inequality levels are higher than those of the later two periods. It should, however, be mentioned that entropies of this period have been calculated at current prices. Even though the entropy of any given year is independent of prices, a comparison of inequality levels between two years is problematic. The fluctuations could have been the result of diverse price movements

Table 4.8A. Entropy estimates at constant prices for 30 provinces (at 1978 prices).[a]

Year	GRP	Primary	Industry	Infrastructure	Services
1978	15.70	1.23	37.81	13.55	22.88
1979	14.26	1.43	37.38	12.21	23.70
1980	14.09	1.53	37.74	12.74	25.17
1981	13.36	1.61	37.07	12.40	21.59
1982	13.01	1.68	36.65	11.87	22.50
1983	12.53	1.67	35.42	12.25	21.33
1984	12.14	1.70	33.93	13.77	18.65

Note: [a]Due to limited data availability, Hainan and Jiangxi provinces are removed for 1978–1984 data.
Source: China National Bureau of Statistics, *Statistical Yearbooks* (published annually).

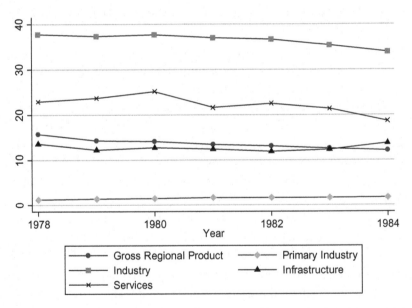

Figure 4.5. Time trend of entropy estimates by sectors from 1978 to 1984.

Table 4.8B. Entropy estimates at current prices for 30 provinces.[a]

Year	GRP	Primary	Secondary	Tertiary
1952	10.75	4.44	45.95	26.67
1953	14.19	3.86	51.66	32.88
1954	13.72	4.80	47.54	29.93
1955	11.42	3.57	43.23	26.12
1956	12.57	3.78	40.66	26.61
1957	12.25	2.78	41.46	24.07
1958	14.39	2.75	40.65	18.89
1959	19.34	3.37	44.49	18.23
1960	24.34	3.92	50.47	18.79
1961	15.34	3.67	43.11	17.55
1962	12.48	3.22	43.96	15.78
1963	13.68	4.31	44.66	15.71
1964	13.14	2.97	41.64	16.08
1965	12.37	2.02	38.24	16.56
1966	12.55	2.57	37.32	16.33
1967	10.74	1.83	35.82	14.75
1968	13.40	1.93	45.25	17.54
1969	14.90	1.55	43.64	17.85
1970	14.94	1.71	39.34	16.82
1971	14.13	1.39	36.02	16.10
1972	14.16	1.87	35.67	15.52
1973	15.05	1.64	36.55	16.93
1974	17.08	1.81	42.57	18.40
1975	16.51	1.47	37.99	19.66
1976	16.73	1.53	39.73	19.23
1977	15.45	1.36	34.12	18.38

Note: [a]The province of Hainan (1952–1977) does not have any available data and hence is removed from the dataset.
Source: CSO, Directorates of Economics & Statistics of respective State Governments (Ministry of Statistics and Programme Implementation).

in regions affecting regional shares. The fluctuations might also have been caused by interregional migration that would make regional population shares unstable. The price indices for sectors are not available for this period. But it is possible to get GRP figures for the regions in real terms.

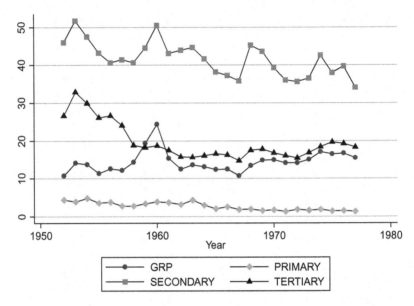

Figure 4.6.   Time trend of entropy estimates by sectors from 1952 to 1977.

Table 4.8C.   Entropy estimates for GRP at 1952 prices for 30 provinces.

1952	1953	1954	1955	1956	1957	1958
10.75	10.18	9.97	9.28	8.45	7.90	7.64
1959	1960	1961	1962	1963	1964	1965
7.16	6.79	4.88	5.40	5.42	5.37	4.95
1966	1967	1968	1969	1970	1971	1972
4.96	4.69	4.29	4.63	4.90	4.99	5.15
1973	1974	1975	1976	1977		
5.19	4.91	5.11	5.20	5.20		

Entropies calculated from real GRP values at 1952 prices for 30 provinces are reported in Table 4.8C. The levels of regional inequality from constant price data are much lower than that from the current price data, but the fluctuations in the two series are similar. Studies on income distribution and social stratification for the period before the market reforms in 1978 have produced many different opinions about the degree of inequality in China. There has been little reliable quantitative data for this period for various reasons including local and regional reports that were exaggerated, inaccurate, or even contrived for political reasons. However, many researchers agree that Maoist China was far more inegalitarian than official statistics revealed. They stress the impact of "back door" activities and corruption of senior cadres that enabled them to receive unofficial and unrecorded benefits from their position within the redistribution system. Studies also stressed the impact of poor economic policies of the Maoist period that exacerbated poverty in rural areas and created inequalities, but served no rational economic purpose. Many researchers would also agree that the post-1978 reforms have simultaneously reduced poverty and increased inequality. Many argue that these new forms of inequality are functional and are simply the price that China must pay for greater efficiency, economic development, and modernization (Griffin and Zha, 1993).

The contribution of each sector of the Chinese economy to the regional inequality in GRP has been estimated in Table 4.9. For what it is worth, the estimated coefficients for the Mao era show positive contributions of all sectors to overall inequality. This pattern changes in the middle period. Though none of the coefficients is significant, primary and industry have negative contributions, while infrastructure and service have positive contributions. The estimates for the modern period show positive contributions of both primary and industry sectors and negative (and statistically significant) contribution of service sector.

Finally, growth–inequality correlation results are presented in Table 4.10. There is no significant correlation between growth rates and inequality during the Mao era, which achieved neither rapid growth nor an equitable income distribution. In the middle period, primary sector inequality has significantly contributed to growth. In the modern period, all correlation coefficients are significant. Only the industrial sector inequality contributes positively to growth, whereas inequality levels in primary, infrastructure, and service have had adverse effects on growth rates.

4.3. Brazil

Post-colonial Brazil has a long history, a part of which has been described in Chapter 2. Over the past three decades, Brazil has emerged as South America's fastest growing economy after deciding to give up import

Table 4.9. Regression (with constraints[a]) results.

	Time period: 1952–1977 dependent variable: ln (entropy of GRP)		Time period: 1978–1984 dependent variable: ln (entropy of GRP)	Time period: 1984–2010 dependent variable: ln (entropy of GRP)
ln (entropy of primary)	0.32[b] (3.23)	ln (entropy of primary)	−0.12 (−0.01)	0.45[b] (14.29)
ln (entropy of secondary)	0.51[b] (2.14)	ln (entropy of industry)	−0.73 (−0.02)	1.13[b] (9.99)
ln (entropy of tertiary)	0.15 (0.45)	ln (entropy of infrastructure)	0.83 (0.01)	−0.08 (−0.28)
		ln (entropy of service)	1.02 (0.06)	−0.49[c] (−1.95)
REPS	500	REPS	500	500
Root-mean-square error	0.28	Root-mean-square error	0.05	0.06

Note: Figures in the parenthesis are z scores. Standard errors are obtained through bootstrapping.
Seed = 10,101; REPS = Number of repetitions.
All 1984–2010 data are in 1984 prices; 1978–1984 data are in 1978 prices, and 1999–2008 data are in 1999–2000 prices;
[a]All slope coefficients add to one;
[b]indicates significance at 1% level of significance;
[c]indicates significance at 5% level of significance;
[d]indicates significance at 10% level of significance.

substitution strategy of industrialization which it pursued for a long time. Brazil experienced many years of strong growth of the economy during the "Brazilian Miracle" of the 1970s. The poverty certainly decreased in those times, but started to grow again with the "Debt Crisis" of the 1980s, which practically nullified the effects of the miracle and this period became known as the lost decade (Garbelotti, 2007). At the end of the 1980s, Brazil had a fiscal deficit, large external debt, hyperinflation, and stagnation. The 21st century came out with a big challenge for the Brazilians. The country has

Table 4.10. Correlation coefficient between entropy measures of inequality and the corresponding annual growth rates.

Category	1952–1977	Category	1978–1984	1984–2010
Primary	−0.03	Primary	0.76[a]	−0.29[a]
Secondary	0.008	Industry	−0.35	0.13[a]
Tertiary	0.28	Infrastructure	0.35	−0.23[a]
		Services	−0.36	−0.12[a]

Note: [a]indicates significance at 1% level of significance; [b]indicates significance at 5% level of significance; [c]indicates significance at 10% level of significance.

one of the highest income inequalities, even if compared with the poorest countries. The taxation system, very regressive, not only helps to keep the *status quo* but also increases the concentration itself. In 2004, the PPA 2004–2007, the strategic plan of government, stated the social inclusion and the reduction of social inequalities as its first important objective. For Brazil, the growth of economy appears as the second mega objective. In fact, since there are complementarities between economic growth and the reduction of inequality to reduce poverty, Brazil has been focusing on a wide range of social inclusion programs, which seem to have reduced inequality and poverty.

At the beginning of the 1990s, the Washington Consensus recommendations were spread out all over the developing countries and Brazil was no exception. Brazil implemented trade and capital liberalization, privatization, flexible exchange rates, and inflation targets (Hasenclever and Paranhos, 2009). Table 4.11 provides the annual average growth rates in

Table 4.11. Annual average gross value added (GVA) growth rates (%).

1950–1960	1960–1970	1970–1980	1980–1990	1990–1995	1995–2009
10.4	8.2	12.9	1.7	3.3	3.1

Source: IBGE in partnership with State Statistical Organizations, State Government Departments and the Superintendence of the Manaus Free Trade Zone (SUFRAMA).

real terms during 1950–2009, which shows reasonably high growth rates till 1980. In 1981–1983, Brazil suffered its worst recession on record, certainly the most severe in the 20th century, as GDP fell 4.9% from its peak in 1980. Massive trade surpluses, the strong recovery of the United States economy in 1984 and the fall in international interest rates made possible a return to current account equilibrium in 1984–1985. There was recovery in the level of economic activity — with GDP growing at 7% on average in 1984–1985 — but yearly inflation doubled again to reach the 200% yearly mark. During 1985, the first year of civilian government after the 1964 military coup, attempts to control inflation based on contractionary monetary and fiscal policies failed. The stage was set for the adoption of a long succession of failed heterodox stabilization plans between 1986 and 1991 until the real plan of 1993–1994 successfully reduced yearly inflation to single digit numbers on a sustained basis (Abreu, 2008 and Table 2.3 of Chapter 2).

The period between 1980 and 1994 should be seen as a transitional period following a severe balance of payments and debt crisis in the beginning of the 1980s. The most important development of Brazilian commercial policy in the 1990s was the creation of Mercosul, *Mercado Comum do Sul* [Southern Common Market] established by the Treaty of Asunción on March 1991 to include Argentina, Brazil, Paraguay, and Uruguay. This was a development of Brazil's *rapprochement* with Argentina since the mid-1980s (Abreu, 2008). In the recent years, the average growth rates in Brazil have never been high enough to be comparable to those in China or India, though in some years the growth rate has reached high figures, such as 5.8% growth in the first four months of 2008 (*The Economist*, 2008). Table 4.12 has the growth rates by sectors during 1995–2004, clearly showing the dominance of agriculture and mining. Entropy estimates of regional inequality in Brazil for 27 federation units for 1995–2009 are reported in Table 4.13 and graphed in Figure 4.7. Regional disparities have a declining trend in GVA as well as in all sectors except in primary. Very high inequality in mining must have been due to the location factor, but it shows a declining trend from 2006. In the case of Brazil, there seems to be a good correlation between regional inequality and personal income inequality, measured by Gini coefficient. Brazil had faced an economic crisis in the 1980s and according to the estimates available from David

Table 4.12. Annual average growth rates (%) by sectors (industry of origin).[a]

	1995–2009 (at 1995 prices)
Primary	4.2
Mining and extraction	4.77
Industry	1.13
Construction	2.16
Utilities	3.28
Services	3.46
GVA	3
Population	1.98

Note: [a]*Primary* refers to agriculture and farming. *Industry* includes all manufacturing and processing units and *utilities* refers to production and distribution of electricity, gas, water and sewage, and urban cleaning. *Services* include the following categories: commerce; financial intermediation, insurance, pension and related services; public administration, health, education, and social security; and other services.
Source: IBGE in partnership with State Statistical Organizations, State Government Departments and the SUFRAMA.

Rockefeller Center for Latin American Studies, Harvard University, Gini coefficient increased from 0.574 in 1981 to 0.625 in 1989, after which it has shown a decline during 1993–2004.[1] According to Garbelotti (2007), income distribution in Brazil has improved since 1993 and consistently from 2003. The main reason for this improvement in income distribution is the reduction of poverty, besides the fact that some decrease in the income of the richest people was observed. Among the main reasons for this reduction in income disparity are lower food prices, improvements in scholarships (Bolsa Escola program) and mainly the advances in social programs, social welfare incomes, and a real increase in the minimum wage. The World Bank study (2001) has made an assessment of

---

[1] ReVista, Harvard Review of Latin America, Spring 2007.

Table 4.13.   Entropy estimates for 27 federation units during 1995–2009 (at 1995 prices).

	GVA	Primary	Industry	Mining and extraction	Construction	Utilities	Services
1995	15.44	19.42	29.44	61.00	12.48	22.11	19.58
1996	14.58	21.85	27.49	62.28	13.01	22.56	18.42
1997	14.67	21.29	27.35	62.34	11.17	22.41	18.45
1998	14.76	22.31	26.07	64.36	10.44	21.84	18.80
1999	14.16	25.53	24.19	70.28	10.20	21.19	18.07
2000	12.98	27.75	24.91	82.90	8.83	19.90	16.36
2001	12.65	23.23	25.04	84.92	8.46	15.67	15.99
2002	11.45	23.72	23.14	93.49	8.40	13.38	14.75
2003	11.19	29.18	23.56	96.36	8.80	10.18	14.17
2004	10.61	33.07	23.42	89.56	8.13	9.08	13.40
2005	10.81	29.75	23.50	108.63	7.11	9.22	13.59
2006	10.78	22.17	22.85	123.44	6.00	7.63	13.54
2007	10.70	27.58	23.79	116.87	5.42	8.11	13.25
2008	10.14	33.10	23.16	114.25	5.61	8.60	13.07
2009	10.27	31.94	23.16	99.68	5.30	7.59	12.96

Source: IBGE in partnership with State Statistical Organizations, State Government Departments and the SUFRAMA.

Bolsa Escola program whose objective is to give cash grants to poor families with school-age (7- to 14-year-olds) children. These grants are given on the condition that the children attend school a minimum number of days per month. These programs began in 1995 at the municipal level in Campinas and the Federal District of Brasilia. By 1999, there were 60 programs in operation in various urban municipalities. Over the same period, and with design similar to the Bolsa Escola programs, two major Federal Programs (FGRM-Fundo de Garantia da Renda Mínima and PETI-Programa de Erradicação do Trabalho Infantil) have been instituted. By the end of 2000, PETI's coverage had reached close to 400,000 children, while FGRM had a coverage estimated at 2 million households. Recently, the Brazilian Government has moved to scale-up (to reach all municipalities with the worst human development indicators by 2002) and integrate

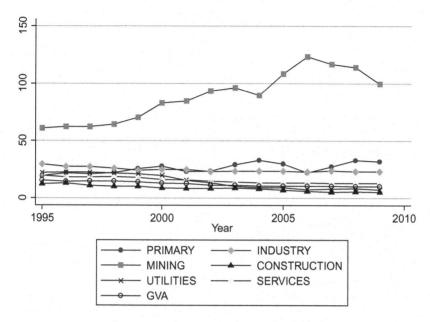

Figure 4.7. Time trend of entropy estimates by sectors from 1995 to 2009.

the FGRM and PETI cash-grant initiatives under one coherent program, the Alvorada program. These programs have four objectives. First, they hope to *increase educational attainment* among today's children and thus *reduce future poverty*. Second, by restricting the grants to the current poor, the programs aim to *reduce current poverty*. Third, by requiring children in beneficiary households to have minimum attendance in school, the programs aim to *reduce child labor*. Last, an implicit objective is that by providing income support to poor families, they *act as a partial safety net* — that is, they prevent these families from falling further into poverty in the event of an adverse shock. Based on existing evidence, the World Bank report finds that the Bolsa Escola programs are appropriately designed and well administered. They have a role to play in the larger social assistance strategy of Brazil. They are likely to remain successful because they enjoy broad support in the government as well as in civil society. The report only raises some concerns regarding future replication or expansion of these programs.

Table 4.14.   Regression (with constraints[a]) results.

	Time period: 1995–2009 dependent variable: ln (entropy of GVA)
ln (entropy of primary)	0.03 (0.51)
ln (entropy of industry)	−0.22 (−1.3)
ln (entropy of mining)	−0.009[d] (−0.15)
ln (entropy of construction)	0.009 (0.15)
ln (entropy of utilities)	−0.15[b] (−2.78)
ln (entropy of services)	1.43[b] (8.14)
REPS	500
Root-mean-square error	0.02

Note: Figures in the parenthesis are z scores. Standard errors are obtained through bootstrapping. Seed = 10,101; REPS = Number of repetitions; all 1995–2009 data are in 1995 prices.
[a]All slope coefficients add to one;
[b]indicates significance at 1% level of significance;
[c]indicates significance at 5% level of significance;
[d]indicates significance at 10% level of significance.

The relative contributions of sectors of the Brazilian economy to overall regional inequality are shown in Table 4.14. Although primary sector and construction seem to raise overall inequality, the coefficients are not significant. The biggest contributor to overall inequality is the service sector. Utility and mining have significant negative contributions.

Finally, the correlation results are reported in Table 4.15. Growth in primary and mining contribute positively to inequality, whereas growth in the rest of the sectors has negative contributions to inequality. There is

Table 4.15. Correlation coefficient between entropy measures of inequality and the corresponding annual growth rates.

Category	1995–2009
Primary	0.28
Industry	−0.25
Mining and extraction	0.47[b]
Construction	−0.35[c]
Utilities	−0.38[c]
Services	−0.44[b]
GVA	−0.43[b]

Note: [a]indicates significance at 1% level of significance;
[b]indicates significance at 5% level of significance;
[c]indicates significance at 10% level of significance.

also a negative correlation between overall regional inequality of income and growth rates. Among the BRIC countries, Brazil exhibits perhaps the most interesting development experience in the 21st century, striking the right balance between the growth objective and the social objective of reduction of poverty and inequality.

4.4. Russia

The growth record of the Soviet Union — its initial success and eventual failure — is a joint outcome of the selected growth strategy and the system of central planning, including almost full state ownership of the means of production. The centrally planned system was more effective at the start in mobilizing all needed resources, and directing them to the goals of industrialization and growth. Ofer (1987) has estimated Soviet GNP per capita measured in 1964 US dollar as $300 in 1928, $600 in 1950, $850 in 1960, $1,250 in 1970, and $1,500 in 1980, which shows that central planning produced economic growth. But the system also caused deprivation of households whose consumption shares in GNP steadily fell in the following way: 68% in 1928, 55% in 1950, 53% in 1960, 49% in 1970,

Table 4.16. Annual average growth rates (%) of real macro variables at 2005 prices.

	1970–1980	1980–1990	1990–1998	1998–2010
Real GDP	3.62	2.07	−4.72	6.67
Real GDP per capita	2.75	1.4	−4.72	7.54
Population	0.66	0.58	−0.01	−0.44

Source: World Bank World Development Indicators, International Financial Statistics of the IMF complied by Mathew Shane (mshane@ers.usda.gov).

and 49% in 1980. The system was also characterized by using commands instead of decentralized initiatives: emphasis on fulfillment of quantitative production targets rather than on improvements in quality, technology, and efficiency, routine expansion instead of creativity and rigidity, and "more of the same" instead of flexibility — a very high cost for any change.[2] Table 4.16 shows the decadal growth rates, with the first two decades belonging to the Cold War period. Low growth rates, particularly during 1980–1990, indicate systemic problems that eventually culminated in the collapse of the Soviet system followed by a transition period in which Russia had negative growth of real GDP. The recent high growth phase began in Russia after the financial collapse of 1998.

Sectoral breakdown of GRP in Russia is available only from 2005 from official sources. The sector-wise growth rates are reported in Table 4.17 which shows negative growth rates in primary, construction, utilities, and services. The growth pattern of Russia in the post-Cold War era has remained essentially the same as in the Cold War period. Agriculture has always been the sector that has lagged behind industry and other sectors. It would be interesting to compare Table 4.17 with Table 1 in Ofer (1987, p. 1778), where the value added by agriculture has grown only at the annual rate of 1.8% during 1928–1985 and its growth rate has been negative during 1975–1980 and zero during 1940–1950. Ofer (1987) has reported

---

[2] For an excellent analysis of the Soviet growth experience during 1928–1985, see Ofer (1987).

Table 4.17. Annual average growth rates (%) by sectors (industry of origin).[a]

	2005–2010 (at 2005 prices)
Primary	−1.37
Mining and extraction	0.41
Industry	1.76
Construction	−0.42
Utilities	−0.27
Services	−0.56
Financial services	2.49
GRP	0.88

Note: [a]GRP is the gross regional product. *Primary* refers to agriculture, hunting, and forestry. *Industry* includes all manufacturing and processing units and *utilities* refers to production and distribution of electricity, gas, and water. *Services* include the following categories: wholesale and retail trade; repair of vehicles, motorcycles, products for the home and items of personal use; transport and communications; operations with real estate, rental, and service provision; public administration and military security; social insurance; education; healthcare, and the provision of social services; other communal, social and personal services, and hotels and restaurants.
Source: Federal State Statistics Service, the Russian Federation (GOSKOMSTAT).

that during 1928–1985 the annual average growth rate of 6.2% in mining, manufacturing, and construction combined and 4.3% growth rate in "all other branches".

In a communist regime, one would not expect any significant degree of income disparity, as the wages were administered and the returns to other factors of production were appropriated by the state. But the regional distribution of economic activities could have been fairly unequal in the former Soviet Union. However, we have no evidence to prove that and, at the same time, one would also expect that planned allocation of resources might have achieved a regional balance as one of its objectives. During the

Table 4.18. GRP entropy estimates for 79 provinces of the Russian federation units during 1998–2010 (at 2005 prices).

	1998	1999	2000	2001	2002	2003	2004	2005
GRP	32.44	32.38	34.18	35.07	34.66	34.04	33.27	32.96

	2006	2007	2008	2009	2010
GRP	33.87	34.98	34.93	37.76	35.49

	Primary	Industry	Mining and extraction	Construction	Utilities	Services	Financial services
2005	34.92	30.22	36.40	37.02	45.06	33.85	60.96
2006	38.13	34.43	42.83	31.40	36.65	40.60	55.30
2007	40.62	38.05	48.20	37.88	41.43	34.66	431.56
2008	36.34	36.18	48.53	36.23	35.18	34.84	86.37
2009	39.34	38.04	45.96	44.68	36.59	36.84	94.82
2010	43.44	40.97	46.99	37.61	34.61	36.15	39.18

Source: Federal State Statistics Service, the Russian Federation (GOSKOMSTAT).

transition of Russia to a market economy, it is only natural for the markets to allocate resources in accordance with the principle of profitability and efficiency and this is likely to cause a great deal of regional imbalance. The entropy estimates of regional inequality during 1998–2010 are reported in Table 4.18 and these are graphed in Figure 4.8 from 2005. Russia has the highest levels of regional inequality among the BRIC countries during this period. Regional inequality estimates for sectors are reported from 2005 in the same table. A study of regional inequality in Russia by Galbraith *et al.* (2004), based on Theil's entropy index, shows a clearly rising trend during 1990–2000. Our sample period is different, but we do not find a significantly rising trend in regional inequality, even though the levels are extremely high. Since the high growth phase started in Russia in about 2000, it seems that economic growth has moderated the rising inequality of the earlier period. The graphs of regional inequality by sectors show fluctuations during 2005–2010, though the regional inequality in GRP remains stable.

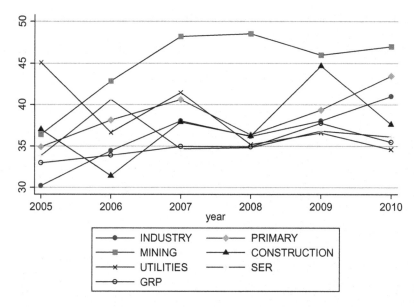

Figure 4.8. Time trend of entropy estimates by sectors from 2005 to 2010.

We have also looked at entropy estimates of regional wage income inequality in Russia as well as regional wage income inequality by sectors during 1990–2000 in order to complete the inequality scenario as far as possible. These are reported in Table 4.19 and graphed in Figure 4.9. The table and graphs capture the rising phase of income inequality in Russia during the transition period in which the growth rate of real GDP and the growth rate of real GDP per capita have been negative.

The contributions of regional disparities in sectors to total regional inequality are reported in Table 4.20, where the entropy estimates for 1990–2000 are measures of wage income inequality. Primary and service sectors have positive and significant contributions to overall wage income inequality during the transition period. The estimates for the second period, 2005–2010, are not comparable to those of the first period, as these are not based on just wage incomes. The contributions of all sectors to overall inequality in the second period are significant. Primary and mining have negative contributions and the rest of the sectors have positive contributions.

Table 4.19.   Wage entropy estimates for 88 provinces of the Russian federation units during 1990–2000.

	GRP	Primary	Industry	Construction	Services	Finance and management services
1990	5.00	2.31	5.88	6.06	5.55	2.33
1991	5.78	3.25	6.65	6.50	6.04	1.92
1992	10.37	5.56	10.44	10.05	12.65	4.65
1993	8.90	5.66	10.78	8.85	8.93	7.88
1994	10.00	7.60	11.08	9.84	9.83	5.40
1995	10.56	8.06	15.51	10.78	8.70	13.61
1996	9.48	7.55	11.62	10.60	8.75	4.34
1997	10.52	8.65	19.74	13.14	10.14	13.93
1998	9.34	10.21	11.70	12.17	9.34	4.17
1999	11.16	8.14	12.19	14.77	9.34	24.14
2000	12.16	8.71	12.40	23.66	11.68	9.59

Source: The entropy numbers are calculated from wage and employment data (of 88 provinces of the Russian Federation from 1990 to 2000) provided by JK Galbraith (Inequality project, University of Texas at Austin). This data set is used to calculate entropy numbers in Galbraith *et al.* (2004). We use a slightly different formula. Entropy $= \Sigma_k(y_k * ln(y_k/p_k))$; where y_k is the share of kth province in the total wage bill and p_k is the share of that province in total employment. We are very grateful to Ludmila Krytynskaia for compiling such a large dataset for a summer research project at Princeton.

The correlation results are in Table 4.21, where primary, construction, and financial services inequality is positively correlated to growth rates in the transition period. In the second period, only the coefficient for the primary sector is positive and significant and the coefficients for the rest are insignificant. We have looked at an alternative source of Russian data to fill the gaps in our study and this source is Galbraith (2004), who has measured regional inequality in terms of wage inequality. Entropy estimates of regional inequality for the period 1990–2000 are reported in Table 4.22. Galbraith's estimates are based on a decomposition of total inequality into "within province" inequality and "between province" inequality. The

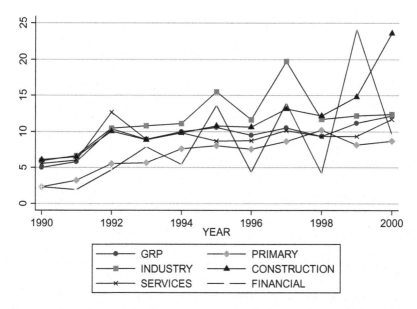

Figure 4.9. Time trends of entropy estimates by sectors from 1990 to 2000.

Table 4.20. Regression (with constraints[a]) results.

	1990–2000 dependent variable: ln (entropy of GRP)	2005–2010 dependent variable: ln (entropy of GRP)
ln (entropy of primary)	0.13[d] (1.79)	−0.55[b] (−4.5)
ln (entropy of industry)	0.17 (0.94)	0.72[b] (6.73)
ln (entropy of mining)		−0.05[d] (−1.65)
ln (entropy of construction)	0.13 (0.36)	0.28[b] (4.73)
ln (entropy of utilities)		0.16[b] (3.17)

(Continued)

Table 4.20.   (*Continued*)

	1990–2000 dependent variable: ln (entropy of GRP)	2005–2010 dependent variable: ln (entropy of GRP)
ln (entropy of services)	0.55[b]	0.43[b]
	(3.0)	(6.47)
REPS	500	500
Root-mean-square error	0.06	0.011

Note: Figures in the parenthesis are z scores. Standard errors are obtained through bootstrapping.
Seed = 10,101; REPS = Number of repetitions; all 1995–2010 data are in 1995 prices.
[a]All slope coefficients add to one. Due to problem of matrix singularity, we have dropped the entropy estimates of financial services as an independent variable for 2005–2010;
[b]indicates significance at 1% level of significance;
[c]indicates significance at 5% level of significance;
[d]indicates significance at 10% level of significance.

Table 4.21.   Correlation coefficient between entropy measures of inequality and the corresponding annual growth rates.

Category	1990–2000	2005–2010
Primary	0.42[a]	0.64[c]
Industry	0.35	0.38
Mining		−0.05
Construction	0.78[c]	−0.56
Utilities		−0.08
Services	0.01	0.09
Financial services	0.61[b]	−0.01
GRP	0.43[a]	−0.58

Note: [a]Indicates significance at 1% level of significance;
[b]indicates significance at 5% level of significance;
[c]indicates significance at 10% level of significance.

Table 4.22. GRP entropy estimates for 79 provinces of the Russian federation units during 1990–2000.

	1990	1991	1992	1993	1994	1995	1996
Theil entropy	3.1	3.5	7	5.9	7.1	7.6	6.8
	1997	1998	1999	2000			
Theil entropy	6.5	6.8	9.5	10.2			
	1990	1991	1992	1993	1994	1995	1996
Real GDP	843.04	800.49	684.17	624.86	546.32	523.68	504.83
	1997	1998	1999	2000			
Real GDP	511.90	484.77	515.79	567.37			
Correlation between inequality and growth	0.58[a]						

[a] indicates significance at 1% level.
Source: Galbraith *et al.* (2004). Real GDP in billion dollars are measured in 2005 dollars.

figures in Table 4.22 are entropy measures of "between province" inequality. The entropy estimates for 1990–2000 show sharply rising interprovincial inequality in Russia. The real GDP figures are also reported in the same table during this period in which the average annual growth rate was negative. The correlation coefficient between annual growth rates and inequality turns out to be positive.

CHAPTER 5

Growth and Inequality in BRIC: Econometric Estimation

5.1. Estimation Method and Framework: The Varying Coefficient Model

The model introduced in Chapter 3 deals with the relationship between economic growth and income inequality, and proposition 1 represents the main prediction of the model. We have distinguished between below average and above average earners in this proposition to show the possibility of income convergence among the below average earners and income divergence among the above average earners in the process of economic growth. To estimate the growth–inequality relationship and allow for heterogeneity of slope coefficients, we employ a random coefficient model, in which the parameters of the model are random and come from a common distribution. When regression coefficients are invariant over time, but vary from one unit or group to another, we can write the model as Equation (5.2). Here, Y_i is a $T \times 1$ vector of observations on the dependent variable, X_i is a $T \times K$ vector of observations on the independent variable (may include lagged dependent variables), ε_i is a $T \times 1$ vector of stochastic disturbances, and β_i is a $N \times 1$ vectors of parameters to be estimated. T is the total number of time periods in the dataset and N is the number of groups/regions.[1]

$$Y_i = X_i \beta_i + \varepsilon_i \qquad (5.1)$$
$$i = 1, 2, \ldots, N.$$

The random coefficient model assumes that the parameters β_i exhibit some similarity, typically $\beta_i = \beta + \eta_i$. Vector β can be viewed as the common

---

[1] For this study we have divided the data into two groups. For the below average workers, $i = 0$ and for the above average workers, $i = 1$.

mean coefficient vector and η_i as the individual deviation from the common mean β. We utilize the methodology of Swamy (1970) to obtain the generalized least squares (GLS) estimates of β_i. Swamy (1970) assumes that $E\eta_i = 0$, $E\eta_i\eta_i' = \Theta$ $(i = 1, \ldots, N)$ and $E\eta_i\eta_j' = 0$ $(i \neq j)$. In addition, the error structure of the model is such that, $E\varepsilon_i = 0$ and $E\varepsilon_i\varepsilon_j' = \sigma_{ij}\Omega_{ij}$, which allows heteroskedastic, first-order autoregressive and mutually correlated errors. The GLS estimator is a matrix weighted average of the least-squares estimator for each cross-sectional unit, with the weighted inversely proportional to their covariance matrices.[2] The GLS estimator $\hat{\beta}$ of β is

$$\hat{\beta} = (X'\hat{\Phi}^{-1}X)^{-1}(X'\hat{\Phi}^{-1}Y), \tag{5.2}$$

where, $\hat{\Phi}$ is the estimate of Φ which has $X_i\Theta X_i' + \sigma_{ii}\Omega_{ii}$ on the diagonal and $\sigma_{ij}\Omega_{ij}$ off the diagonal.

5.2. Framework, Data, and Results

Proposition 1 discusses how the relationship between rate of growth of income (Y_{it}) and inequality depends upon the initial income distribution. Income diverges for the above average earners and converges for the below average earners. To test this proposition, we divide our dataset into two groups: below average $(k = 0)$ above average earners $(k = 1)$. The random coefficient model estimates the relationship between growth and the income gap (X_{1it}) for each subgroup. The random coefficient model allows the slope estimates to vary across the groups. To capture the effect of macroeconomic variables, such as savings rate and technical progress, we include another independent variable, X_{2t}, the growth rate of aggregate income of the country (calculated as the sum of regional incomes) in year t.

Swamy's (1970) methodology is used to obtain the GLS estimates of β_1 and β_2 from the following population regression function:

$$Y_{it} = \beta_0 + \beta_1 X_{1it} + \beta_2 X_{2t} + \varepsilon_{it}; \quad (k = 0 \text{ or } 1).$$

---

[2] Refer to Swamy (1970), for a detailed explanation of the random-coefficient models.

From the random coefficient model, we can estimate a slope coefficient for each independent variable, for every subgroup. Thus, we will be able to estimate β_1 or $\partial Y_{it}/\partial X_{1it}$, the relationship between the ith region's annual growth rate in year t (Y_{it}) and the income gap (X_{1it}) for each subgroup, $k = 0$ and $k = 1$. Further, we will be able to estimate β_2 or $\partial Y_{it}/\partial X_{2t}$, the relationship between Y_{it} and the growth rate of aggregate income of the country (X_{2t}) for each subgroup ($k = 0, 1$). For each country India, China, Brazil, and Russia, we will look at the relationship between Y_{it} and X_{1it} and the relationship between Y_{it} and X_{2t} for each subgroup ($k = 0, 1$).

In the random coefficient model, the dependent variable Y_{it}, is the ith region's annual growth rate in year t.[3] In our regression model, the first independent variable (X_{1it}) could be the difference between the ith region's income in year t and the average income of all regions in year t. However, in order to make the variables in the regression model comparable (Y_{it} is a percentage change and X_{1it} is the regional income in local currency of the country), we redefine X_{1it} as a percentage of income. Thus, X_{1it} measures the income gap in percentage. The coefficient of X_{1it}, ($\partial Y_{it}/\partial X_{1it}$) will help us determine if income converges or diverges in each group. The theoretical model also highlights the importance of savings rate and technical progress on the distribution of income. To capture the effect of these macroeconomic variables, we include another independent variable, X_{2t}, the growth rate of aggregate income of the country (calculated as the sum of regional incomes) in year t.

The income of any region in the deprived group ($k = 0$ is less than the average income ($X_{1it} < 0$). For this group, we expect a negative relationship between the income gap and growth rates. According to theory, in this group, the relatively more affluent region (the one with higher value of X_{1it}) will grow at a slower rate (thus, leading to convergence in the deprived group).

The income of any region in the affluent group ($k = 1$) is greater than the average income ($X_{1it} > 0$). For this group, we expect a positive relationship between income and growth rates. In this group, the relatively

---

[3] The region could be a state, province, or federation unit.

more affluent region (the one with higher value of X_{1it}) will grow at a faster rate (thus, leading to income divergence in the affluent group).

The regression model does not need to incorporate any measure of inequality. Our purpose is to determine if there is convergence or divergence in the two income groups ($k = 0$ for the deprived group and $k = 1$ for the affluent group). Inequality trends are discussed in detail in previous chapters.

5.3. Case of India

We start our analysis with the case of India. We look at the data for 31 states and union territories during the time period: 1980–2008. The time period is divided into three subperiods: 1980–1997, 1993–2001, and 1999–2008. All data are in real values and each subperiod has a different base year. For some time periods, data for fewer states and union territories are available. Some union territories were created in the 21st century. The data set is obtained from the CSO, Directorates of Economics & Statistics of respective State Governments (Ministry of Statistics and Programme Implementation).[4]

For India, Y_{it} is the growth rate of real NSDP. The exogenous variable X_{1it} is the difference between real NSDP of the ith state at year t and the average real NSDP of all states at year t (as a percentage of NSDP of the ith state at year t); and X_{2t} is the annual growth rate of the sum of NSDP of all states in year t.

5.3.1. *Discussion of results for India*

Although any measure of inequality (such the Gini index or the Theil entropy index) is not an exogenous variable of the regression model, the estimated results will shed some light on income convergence or divergence in each group, the deprived ($k = 0$) and the affluent ($k = 1$). The regression results for India are presented in Table 5.1.

---

[4] We are very grateful to P Bhanumati (Director, Central Statistical Office), Ashish Kumar (Additional Director General, Ministry of Statistics & Programme Implementation), PC Mohanan (Deputy Director General, Ministry of Statistics & Programme Implementation) for all state-level data (beyond what is available online).

Table 5.1.   Regression results for India.

Dependent variable: Y_{it}

	1980–1997 to 1993–1994	1993–2001 to 2004–2005	1999–2008 to 2007–2008
$k = 0$			
X_{1it}	−0.015[a]	0.004	0.004
	(0.000)	(0.088)	(0.035)
X_{2t}	0.604[a]	0.013	0.581[a]
	(0.062)	(0.205)	(0.054)
Constant	1.758[a]	5.98[a]	3.229[a]
	(0.503)	(1.58)	(0.645)
$k = 1$			
X_{1it}	1.937[a]	−4.00[b]	−1.375[c]
	(0.748)	(−1.65)	(0.791)
X_{2t}	1.14[a]	1.00[b]	1.062[a]
	(0.219)	(0.445)	(0.196)
Constant	−1.375	3.00	0.5
	(1.252)	(1.99)	(1.793)
Number of observations	399	210	256
Number of $k = 1$	174	85	109
Percentage of $k = 1$	43.6%	40.4%	42.5%
Wald chi-square		0.75	18.79[a]
(p value)		(0.686)	(0.000)

Note: Figures in the parenthesis are standard errors.
All 1980–1997 data are in 1980–1981 prices, 1993–2001 data are in 1993–1994 prices, and 1999–2008 data are in 1999–2000 prices;
[a] indicates significance at 1% level of significance;
[b] indicates significance at 5% level of significance;
[c] indicates significance at 10% level of significance.

First, we look at estimated coefficients for the deprived group ($k = 0$). The income of a state in this group is less than the average income ($X_{1it} < 0$). According to proposition 1 of the theoretical model, the relatively richer state in this group grows at a slower rate, thus, leading to income convergence. We find data evidence to support income convergence in the deprived group only during the time period 1980–1997.

Only in this time period, the coefficient of X_{1it} is negative and significant. During the time periods: 1993–2005 and 1999–2008, the estimated coefficient of X_{1it} is positive, but not statistically significant.

Next, we look at estimated results for the affluent group ($k = 1$). The income of a state in this group is greater than the average income ($X_{1it} > 0$). According to proposition 1 of the theoretical model, the relatively richer state in this group grows at a faster rate, thus, leading to income divergence. We find data evidence to support income divergence in the affluent group only during the time period 1980–1994. Only in this time period, the coefficient of X_{1it} is positive and significant. During the time periods 1993–2005 and 1999–2008, the estimated coefficient of X_{1it} is negative and significant. Contrary to the expectations of the theoretical model, we find income is converging among the states in the affluent group. However, these estimates are capable of partly explaining the trends in regional income inequality in India, measured by the Theil index and reported in Tables 4.2, 4.3, and 4.4 in Chapter 4. The entropy measures for NSDP are reported in these tables. The period of 1980–1981 to 1993–1994 is marked by a steady increase in regional inequality due to a significant but quantitatively small income convergence among below average states and a significant and quantitatively large income divergence among above average states. Regional inequality also shows slightly rising trend during 1993–1994 to 2000–2001 and no significant change during 1999–2008. There is no doubt that this deceleration in the rising inequality trend of the first period has been caused by significant and substantive income convergence among the above average earners during the second two subperiods of the random coefficient regression estimates.

The relationship between the growth rate of national income and growth rate of state income is positive for both groups. The estimated coefficient of X_{2t} is positive for the deprived group as well as the affluent group for all time periods: 1980–1997, 1993–2005, and 1999–2008. The estimated slope coefficient is also significant for most time periods. This shows that the economic growth at the national level has benefitted all states, irrespective of their levels of affluence or deprivation.

5.4. Case of China

We look at the data for 30 provinces during the time period: 1952–1977, 1978–1984, and 1985–2010. All data are in real values and each subperiod has a different base year. The data set is obtained from the *Statistical Yearbooks* published yearly by the China National Bureau of Statistics.[5]

Y_{it} is the growth rate of real GRP. The exogenous variable X_{1it} is the difference between real GRP of the ith province at year t and the average real GRP of all provinces at year t (as a percentage of real GRP of the ith state at year t) and X_{2t} is the annual growth rate of the sum of GRP of all states in year t.

5.4.1. Discussion of results for China

First, we look at estimated coefficients for the deprived group ($k = 0$). The income of a state in this group is less than the average income ($X_{1it} < 0$). According to proposition 1 of the theoretical model, the relatively richer state in this group grows at a slower rate, thus, leading to income convergence. We do not find data evidence to support income convergence in the deprived group during any time period. In contrast, during all time periods: 1952–1977, 1978–1984, and 1985–2010, we find support for income divergence in the deprived group.

Next, we look at estimated results for the affluent group ($k = 1$). The income of a state in this group is greater than the average income ($X_{1it} > 0$). According to proposition 1 of the theoretical model, the relatively richer state in this group grows at a faster rate, thus, leading to income divergence. We find data evidence to support income divergence in the affluent group only during the time period 1952–1977. Only in this time period, the coefficient of X_{1it} is positive and significant. During the period 1978–1984, the estimated coefficient of X_{1it} is negative but not significant. During 1985–2010, the estimated coefficient is negative and significant, thus, indicating an income convergence in the affluent group in this subperiod. Referring back to Chapter 4, Tables 4.8, 4.8A, 4.8B, and 4.8C have

---

[5] http://www.stats.gov.cn/english/.

entropy measures of regional income inequality in China. We may ignore Table 4.8B, because GRP in these estimates of entropy are in current prices. All these tables show declining trends in regional inequality in China except during 1991–2002. As in the case of India, the uniform transfer model does not fit perfectly, but is capable of partially explaining the inequality trends. Table 5.2 shows income divergence for both the above average and below average groups during 1952–1977, which does not quite

Table 5.2. Regression results for China.

Dependent variable: Y_{it}

	1952–1977	1978–1984	1985–2010
$k = 0$			
X_{1it}	0.048[a]	0.056	0.035[a]
	(0.012)	(0.122)	(0.000)
X_{2t}	0.790[a]	0.984[a]	0.972[a]
	(0.037)	(0.050)	(0.020)
Constant	−0.066	−0.054	0.649[a]
	(0.193)	(0.173)	(0.156)
$k = 1$			
X_{1it}	1.5[a]	−0.312	−0.921[a]
	(0.429)	(0.869)	(0.255)
X_{2t}	1.125[a]	0.914[a]	0.989[a]
	(0.111)	(0.144)	(0.020)
Constant	−0.421[c]	0.375	0.308[c]
	(0.224)	(0.632)	(0.183)
Number of observations	750	174	780
Number of $k = 1$	325	78	350
Percentage of $k = 1$	45.1%	44.8%	44.8%
Wald chi-square	101.25[a]	0.75	18.79[a]
(p value)	(0.000)	(0.686)	(0.000)

Note: Figures in the parenthesis are standard errors.
All 1952–1977 data are in 1952 prices, 1978–1984 data are in 1978 prices, and 1985–2010 data are in 1985 prices;
[a] indicates significance at 1% level of significance;
[b] indicates significance at 5% level of significance;
[c] indicates significance at 10% level of significance.

explain why regional inequality declined during this period. However, significant income convergence among above average provinces combined to a certain degree of income divergence among the below average provinces is capable of explaining declining inequality during the overall period of 1978–2010.

Similar to the case for India, in China, the estimated coefficient of X_{2t} is positive for all time periods: 1952–1977, 1978–1984, and 1985–2010 (and significant for all subperiods). This result holds for both the deprived as well as the affluent groups. For both groups of states, the growth rate of national income and growth rate of any region's income are positively related. The regression results for Brazil are presented in Table 5.3.

5.5. Case of Brazil

We look at the data for 28 federation units during the time period: 1996–2010. All data are in real values and with 1995 as the base year. The data set is obtained from the IBGE in partnership with State Statistical Organizations, State Government Departments and SUFRAMA.[6]

Y_{it} is the growth rate of real GVA of the ith federation unit in year t. The exogenous variable X_{1it} is the difference between real GVA of the ith federation unit at year t and the average real GVA of all federation units at year t (as a percentage of real GVA of the ith federation unit at year t); and X_{2t} is the annual growth rate of the sum of GRP of all states in year t.

5.5.1. Discussion of results for Brazil

First, we look at estimated coefficients for the deprived group ($k = 0$). The income of a state in this group is less than the average income ($X_{1it} < 0$). According to proposition 1 of the theoretical model, the relatively richer state in this group grows at a slower rate, thus, leading to income convergence. During the years 1995–2010, we find support for income divergence in the deprived group. The estimated coefficient of X_{1i} is significant and positive.

---

[6] http://www.ibge.gov.br/english/.

Table 5.3. Regression results for Brazil.

Dependent Variable: Y_{it}

	1995–2010
$k = 0$	
X_{1it}	7.947[a]
	(1.761)
X_{2t}	1.076[a]
	(0.075)
Constant	−1[b]
	(0.412)
$k = 1$	
X_{1it}	7.863[a]
	(1.761)
X_{2t}	0.906[a]
	(0.079)
Constant	1.625[a]
	(0.583)
Number of observations	364
Number of $k = 1$	147
Percentage of $k = 1$	40.3%
Wald chi-square	86.53[a]
(p value)	(0.000)

Note: Figures in the parenthesis are standard errors.
All 1995–2010 data are in 1995 prices;
[a] indicates significance at 1% level of significance;
[b] indicates significance at 5% level of significance;
[c] indicates significance at 10% level of significance.

Next, we look at estimated results for the affluent group ($k = 1$). The income of a state in this group is greater than the average income ($X_{1it} > 0$). According to proposition 1 of the theoretical model, the relatively richer state in this group grows at a faster rate, thus, leading to income divergence. We find data evidence to support income divergence in the affluent group during the time period 1995–2010. The coefficient of X_{1it} is positive and significant. Table 4.13, giving entropy measures based on Brazil's GVA at constant prices, shows a declining trend in regional inequality during

1995–2009, even though the data show increases in inequality in some years. Since the random coefficient estimates show income divergence among both the below average and above average groups, the uniform transfer model does not fit very well in the case of Brazil. The only explanation that can be provided is that income transfers in Brazil have significantly deviated from the uniformity rule that is assumed in the model.

For the deprived and affluent groups, the estimated coefficient of X_{2t} is positive and significant during 1995–2010. For both groups of states, the growth rate of national income and growth rate of any region's income are positively related.

5.6. Case of Russia

We look at the real income data for 79 provinces during the time period: 1998–2010 (at 2005 prices) and wage data for 88 provinces during 1990–2000 (at 1990 prices). GRP data are obtained from the Federal State Statistics Service of the Russian Federation (GOSKOMSTAT). For the wage data, we are very grateful to J. K. Galbraith (Inequality project, University of Texas at Austin) and Ludmila Krytynskaia for compiling such a large dataset for a summer research project at Princeton.

Y_{it} is the growth rate of real GRP. The exogenous variable X_{1it} is the difference between real GRP of the ith province at year t and the average real GRP of all provinces at year t (as a percentage of real GRP of the ith state at year t) and X_{2t} is the annual growth rate of the sum of GRP of all states in year t. Table 5.4 has the regression results for Russia.

5.6.1. Discussion of results for Russia

First, we look at estimated coefficients for the deprived group ($k = 0$). The income of a state in this group is less than the average income ($X_{1it} < 0$). According to proposition 1 of the theoretical model, the relatively richer state in this group grows at a slower rate, thus, leading to income convergence. During the years 1998–2010, we find support for income divergence in the deprived group. The estimated coefficient of X_{1i} is significant and positive. During the years 1990–2000, the estimated coefficient of X_{1i} is positive, but not statistically significant.

Table 5.4.   Regression results for Russia.

Dependent variable: Y_{it}

	1990–2000[a]	1998–2010
$k = 0$		
X_{1it}	0.345	90.375[b]
	(0.311)	(4.437)
X_{2t}	0.874[b]	0.953[b]
	(0.011)	(0.031)
Constant	17.903[c]	0.792[b]
	(8.251)	(0.222)
$k = 1$		
X_{1it}	96[b]	116.25[b]
	(40.2)	(7.692)
X_{2t}	1.093[b]	1.081[b]
	(0.098)	(0.043)
Constant	−6	−0.75[d]
	(13.933)	(0.434)
Number of observations	880	948
Number of $k = 1$	281	452
Percentage of $k = 1$	31.9%	47.6%
Wald chi-square	2710[b]	290.33[b]
(*p* value)	(0.000)	(0.000)

Note: Figures in the parenthesis are standard errors.
All 1998–2010 data are in 1995 prices; calculations for the period 1990–2000 are based on wage and employment data.
[a] These calculations are based on the wage and employment data provided by JK Galbraith (Inequality project, University of Texas at Austin) for 88 provinces of the Russian Federation;
[b] indicates significance at 1% level of significance;
[c] indicates significance at 5% level of significance;
[d] indicates significance at 10% level of significance.

Next, we look at estimated results for the affluent group ($k = 1$). The income of a state in this group is greater than the average income ($X_{1it} > 0$). According to proposition 1 of the theoretical model, the relatively richer state in this group grows at a faster rate, thus, leading to income divergence. We find data evidence to support income divergence in the affluent group during the both time periods: 1990–2000 and 1998–2010. The GRP entropy estimates for Russia, reported in Table 4.18, show no significant time trend in regional inequality. However, wage inequality during 1990–2000 in Table 4.19 or Galbraith's estimates of GRP entropies during 1990–2000, reported in Table 4.22, show steadily rising regional inequality in Russia. The random coefficient estimates showing divergence in both below average and above average groups would perfectly explain this rising inequality trend.

Similar to the cases of India, China, and Brazil, the estimated coefficient of X_{2t} is positive and significant for all time periods: 1990–2000 and 1998–2010. This result holds for both the deprived as well as the affluent groups. For both groups of states, the growth rate of national income and growth rate of any region's income are positively related.

5.7. Regression with Low versus High Inequality Subgroups

We now reclassify the dataset of each country (for each sub period) by dividing the data into two different subgroups: low inequality ($k = 0$) and high inequality ($k = 1$).[7] For each country India (Table 5.5), China (Table 5.6), Brazil (Table 5.7), and Russia (Table 5.8), we look at the relationship among Y_{it} (ith region's annual growth rate in year t) and X_{1it} (the income gap) and Y_{it} and X_{2t} (growth rate of aggregate income of the country) for each inequality subgroup.

For the case of India, the estimate of coefficient of X_{1it} from the random coefficients model is significant only for the high inequality group. We see income divergence for this group during 2004–2011. Only during 1980–1994 do we see an income divergence for the high inequality group. However, the estimated coefficient of X_{1it} is negative and insignificant. The relationship between growth of regional income and growth of national income ($\partial Y_{it}/\partial X_{2t}$) is significant and positive for all time periods and groups.

For the case of China, the estimate of coefficient of X_{1it} from the random coefficients model is significant only for the high inequality group

---

[7] We sort the data in increasing order of inequality according to the Theil entropy index and then divide the entire dataset into two groups.

Table 5.5.   Regression results for India.

Dependent Variable: Y_{it}

	1980–1999	1993–2001	1999–2008
$k = 0$ (low inequality)			
X_{1it}	−0.007	0.015	−0.02
	(0.018)	(0.035)	(0.019)
X_{2t}	0.812^a	1.0^c	0.716^a
	(0.208)	(0.567)	(0.138)
Constant	0.875	0.5	2.085
	(1.012)	(3.576)	(1.391)
$k = 1$ (high inequality)			
X_{1it}	−0.005	0.011	0.099^a
	(0.020)	(0.035)	(0.042)
X_{2t}	0.875^a	0.187	2.343^a
	(0.144)	(0.459)	(0.351)
Constant	1	5.5^b	−13.5^b
	(1.17)	(2.641)	(6.331)
Wald chi-square	36.39^a	0.89	9.29^a
(p value)	(0.00)	(0.64)	(0.000)

Note: Figures in the parenthesis are standard errors.
All 1980–1997 data are in 1980–1981 prices, 1993–2001 data are in 1993–1994 prices, and 1999–2008 data are in 1999–2000 prices.
^{a} indicates significance at 1% level of significance;
^{b} indicates significance at 5% level of significance;
^{c} indicates significance at 10% level of significance.

during 1952–1977. We see income divergence for this group during this period. Only during 1985–2010 do we see an income divergence for the high inequality group. However, the estimated coefficient of X_{1it} is negative and insignificant. The relationship between growth of regional income and growth of national income ($\partial Y_{it}/\partial X_{2t}$) is significant and positive for all time periods and groups.

For the case of Brazil, the estimate of coefficient of X_{1it} from the random coefficients model is positive and significant for the high ($k = 1$) and low inequality ($k = 0$) groups during 1995–2010. We see income divergence

Table 5.6.   Regression results for China.

Dependent variable: Y_{it}

	1952–1977	1978–1984	1985–2010
$k = 0$			
X_{1it}	0.05	0.0625	0.046
	(0.04)	(0.083)	(0.046)
X_{2t}	1.0^a	0.937^a	1.0^a
	(0.103)	(0.087)	(0.025)
Constant	0.052	0.078	0.273^c
	(0.180)	(0.248)	(0.147)
$k = 1$			
X_{1it}	0.105^a	0.062	−0.035
	(0.042)	(0.067)	(0.041)
X_{2t}	0.781^a	0.968^a	0.968^a
	(0.116)	(0.088)	(0.023)
Constant	0.101	0.062	0.289^c
	(0.181)	(0.247)	(0.147)
Wald chi-square	84.4^a	123.73^a	1925.15^a
(p value)	(0.000)	(0.00)	(0.000)

Note: Figures in the parenthesis are standard errors.
All 1952–1977 data are in 1952 prices, 1978–1984 data are in 1978 prices, and 1985–2010 data are in 1985 prices;
[a] indicates significance at 1% level of significance;
[b] indicates significance at 5% level of significance;
[c] indicates significance at 10% level of significance.

for both groups during this period. The relationship between growth of regional income and growth of national income $(\partial Y_{it}/\partial X_{2t})$ is significant and positive for all groups during 1995–2010.

For the case of Russia, similar to the case of Brazil, the estimate of coefficient of X_{1it} from the random coefficients model is positive and significant for the high $(k = 1)$ and low inequality $(k = 0)$ groups during 1990–2000 and 1998–2010. We see income divergence for both groups during this period. The relationship between growth of regional income and growth of national income $(\partial Y_{it}/\partial X_{2t})$ is significant and positive for all groups during 1990–2000 and 1998–2010.

Table 5.7.   Regression results for Brazil.

Dependent variable: Y_{it}

	1995–2010
$k = 0$	
X_{1it}	10.3^a
	(1.93)
X_{2t}	0.988^a
	(0.075)
Constant	0.285
	(0.35)
$k = 1$	
X_{1it}	18.81^a
	(2.928)
X_{2t}	0.983^a
	(0.075)
Constant	0.275
	(0.35)
Wald chi-square	184.96^a
(*p* value)	(0.000)

Note: Figures in the parenthesis are standard errors.
All 1995–2010 data are in 1995 prices;
^{a} indicates significance at 1% level of significance;
^{b} indicates significance at 5% level of significance;
^{c} indicates significance at 10% level of significance.

5.8.   Regression with Low Growth versus High Growth Subgroups

We now reclassify the dataset of each country (for each subperiod) by dividing the data into two subgroups by regional growth: low growth ($k = 0$) and high growth ($k = 1$).[8]   For each country India (Table 5.9), China (Table 5.10), Brazil (Table 5.11), and Russia (Table 5.12), we look at the

---

[8] We have sort the data in increasing order of regional growth rates and then have divided the entire dataset into two groups.

Table 5.8. Regression results for Russia.

Dependent variable: Y_{it}

	1990–2000	1998–2009
$k = 0$		
X_{1it}	1.754[a]	92.589[a]
	(0.0679)	(3.479)
X_{2t}	1.145[a]	1.01[a]
	(0.030)	(0.032)
Constant	−3.14	0.481[a]
	(8.308)	(0.187)
$k = 1$		
X_{1it}	1.433[b]	92.773[a]
	(0.683)	(3.477)
X_{2t}	0.886[a]	1.008[a]
	(0.065)	(0.032)
Constant	33.875[a]	0.491[a]
	(11.741)	(0.186)
Wald chi-square	55.66[a]	1646.78[a]
(*p* value)	(0.00)	(0.00)

Note: Figures in the parenthesis are standard errors.
All 1998–2010 data are in 1995 prices; calculations for the period 1990–2000 are based on wage and employment data;
[a] indicates significance at 1% level of significance;
[b] indicates significance at 5% level of significance;
[c] indicates significance at 10% level of significance.

relationship between Y_{it} (ith region's annual growth rate in year t) and X_{1it} (the income gap) and the relationship between Y_{it} and X_{2t} (growth rate of aggregate income of the country) for each growth subgroup.

We see mixed results for the case of India. The estimate of coefficient of X_{1it} from the random coefficients model is significant for the high growth group. We see income convergence during 1980–1997 and income divergence during 1999–2008. For the low growth group, the estimated coefficient of X_{1it} is positive and significant during 1993–2005. The relationship between growth of regional income and growth of national income $(\partial Y_{it}/\partial X_{2t})$ is significant and positive for almost all

Table 5.9.   Regression results for India.

Dependent variable: Y_{it}

	1980–1997	1993–2001	1999–2008
$k = 0$ (low growth)			
X_{1it}	0.018	0.054[b]	0.0009
	(0.012)	(0.023)	(0.018)
X_{2t}	0.331[a]	0.354[c]	0.485[a]
	(0.090)	(0.2)	(0.091)
Constant	−0.734	−0.039	0.203
	(0.529)	(1.126)	(0.716)
$k = 1$ (high growth)			
X_{1it}	−0.020[c]	0.016	0.034[c]
	(0.012)	(0.023)	(0.018)
X_{2t}	0.522[a]	−0.2	0.157[c]
	(0.090)	(0.201)	(0.09)
Constant	6.671[a]	12.078[a]	−10.375[a]
	(0.611)	(1.3)	(0.693)
Wald chi-square	16.75[a]	1.55	7.67[b]
(p value)	(0.00)	(0.46)	(0.021)

Note: Figures in the parenthesis are standard errors.
All 1980–1997 data are in 1980–1981 prices, 1993–2001 data are in 1993–1994 prices, and 1999–2008 data are in 1999–2000 prices;
[a] indicates significance at 1% level of significance;
[b] indicates significance at 5% level of significance;
[c] indicates significance at 10% level of significance.

time periods and all subgroups. In the years when Indian economy had low growth, incomes mostly diverged, though not always significantly. But the growth of the national economy has a positive effect on regional incomes, irrespective of high or low growth phases with only one exception.

For the case of China, the estimate of coefficient of X_{1it} from the random coefficients model is significant only during the time period 1985–2010. We see income divergence for the low growth group $(k = 0)$

Table 5.10. Regression results for China.

Dependent variable: Y_{it}

	1952–1977	1978–1984	1985–2010
$k = 0$ (low growth)			
X_{1it}	0.034	0.056	0.032^c
	(0.026)	(0.052)	(0.019)
X_{2t}	0.058	0.762^a	0.599^a
	(0.073)	(0.07)	(0.021)
Constant	−2.351^a	−1.738^a	0.113
	(0.25)	(0.309)	(0.159)
$k = 1$ (high growth)			
X_{1it}	−0.036	0.011	−0.077^a
	(0.026)	(0.052)	(0.020)
X_{2t}	0.888^a	0.345^a	0.789^a
	(0.072)	(0.07)	(0.023)
Constant	2.4^a	3.015	2.289^a
	(0.233)	(0.292)	(0.194)
Wald chi-square	3.34	6.5^b	286.8^a
(p value)	(0.188)	(0.038)	(0.000)

Note: Figures in the parenthesis are standard errors.
All 1952–1977 data are in 1952 prices, 1978–1984 data are in 1978 prices, and 1985–2010 data are in 1985 prices;
^{a}indicates significance at 1% level of significance;
^{b}indicates significance at 5% level of significance;
^{c}indicates significance at 10% level of significance.

and income convergence for the high growth group ($k = 1$) during this period. We find a similar pattern of results for the time period 1952–1977; however, they are not statistically significant. The relationship between growth of regional income and growth of national income ($\partial Y_{it}/\partial X_{2t}$) is significant and positive for almost all time periods and for both groups.

For the case of Brazil, the estimate of coefficient of X_{1it} from the random coefficients model is positive and significant for the high ($k = 1$) and low growth ($k = 0$) groups during 1995–2010. We see income divergence

Table 5.11.   Regression results for Brazil.

Dependent variable: Y_{it}

	1995–2010
$k = 0$ (low growth)	
X_{1it}	4.972[a]
	(1.032)
X_{2t}	0.663[a]
	(0.071)
Constant	−1.6[a]
	(0.433)
$k = 1$ (high growth)	
X_{1it}	7.522[a]
	(1.033)
X_{2t}	0.283[a]
	(0.072)
Constant	5.945[a]
	(0.467)
Wald chi-square	61.00[a]
(p value)	(0.000)

Note: Figures in the parenthesis are standard errors.
All 1995–2010 data are in 1995 prices;
[a]indicates significance at 1% level of significance;
[b]indicates significance at 5% level of significance;
[c]indicates significance at 10% level of significance.

for both groups during this period. The relationship between growth of regional income and growth of national income $(\partial Y_{it}/\partial X_{2t})$ is significant and positive for all groups during 1995–2010.

For the case of Russia, the estimate of coefficient of X_{1it} from the random coefficients model is positive and significant for the high $(k = 1)$ and low growth $(k = 0)$ groups during 1990–2000 and 1998–2010. We see income divergence for both groups during this period. The relationship between growth of regional income and growth of national income $(\partial Y_{it}/\partial X_{2t})$ is significant and positive for all groups during 1990–2000 and 1998–2010.

Table 5.12. Regression results for Russia.

Dependent variable: Y_{it}

	1990–2000	1998–2009
$k = 0$ (low growth)		
X_{1it}	0.248^b	62.765^a
	(0.105)	(3.252)
X_{2t}	0.636^a	0.574^a
	(0.019)	(0.034)
Constant	8.832^b	-2.695^a
	(3.656)	(0.293)
$k = 1$ (high growth)		
X_{1it}	3.027^a	89.835^a
	(0.399)	(3.190)
X_{2t}	0.892^a	0.862^a
	(0.042)	(0.033)
Constant	89.625^a	2.894^a
	(12.368)	(0.265)
Wald chi-square	329.26^a	32.11^a
(*p* value)	(0.00)	(0.00)

Note: Figures in the parenthesis are standard errors. All 1998–2010 data are in 1995 prices; calculations for the period 1990–2000 are based on wage and employment data.
^{a}indicates significance at 1% level of significance;
^{b}indicates significance at 5% level of significance;
^{c}indicates significance at 10% level of significance.

5.9. Regression Results with Low Corruption versus High Corruption Subgroups

We now reclassify the dataset of each country (for each sub period) by dividing the data into two subgroups by an index of corruption: high corruption ($k = 0$) and low corruption ($k = 1$).[9] For each country India (Table 5.13),

---

[9] For the corruption perception index, we collected data from the Transparency International (http://www.transparency.org/). The perception index ranges from 0 to 10–0

China (Table 5.14), Brazil (Table 5.15), and Russia (Table 5.16), we look at the relationship between Y_{it} (ith region's annual growth rate in year t) and X_{1it} (the income gap) and the relationship between Y_{it} and X_{2t} (growth rate of aggregate income of the country) for each corruption subgroup.

The first subgroup ($k = 0$) includes all observations on regions where the degree of government corruption is high. For this group, we expect a positive relationship between the ith region's annual growth rate in year t (Y_{it}) and the income gap (X_{1it}). In this subgroup, values of X_{1it} will be positive in some regions (for regions belonging to the affluent group) and negative in some regions (for regions in the deprived group). In the presence of high corruption, higher the region's income in the affluent group or the deprived group, higher is the gap and faster is the growth rate, thus, leading to income divergence. Note, if the gap is negative, a higher gap for the ith region ($-2>-3$) indicates that region in more affluent among those in the deprived group. The analysis is reversed for the second subgroup ($k = 1$), which includes all observations on regions where the level of corruption is low. For this group, we expect a negative relationship between the ith region's annual growth rate in year t (Y_{it}) and the income gap (X_{1it}). If the government of these regions is not corrupt, it will assist in the transfer of income from the affluent to the deprived, and as a result incomes of the more privileged in the affluent group or the deprived group will grow at a slower rate than the incomes of the less privileged in the affluent group or the deprived group, thus, leading to income convergence.

The corruption perception index is available only for the time period 1995–2010. Hence, we have restricted our estimation to the available years.

First, we look at the first and second columns of the table for India (Table 5.13). The estimate of coefficient of X_{1it} from the random coefficients model is significant only for the high corruption group for time periods: 1995–2001 and 2001–2008. We see income convergence for the high corruption group and income divergence for the low corruption group; however, the estimates for the low corruption group are statistically

representing the highest level of corruption and 10 representing no corruption. We have sort the data in increasing order of the corruption perception index and then have divided the entire dataset into two groups.

Table 5.13. Regression results for India.

Dependent variable: Y_{it}

	Data sorted by Corruption Perception Index		Data sorted by regime change
	1995–1996 to 2000–2001	2000–2001 to 2007–2008	1994–1995 to 2000–2001
$k = 0$ (high corruption)			
X_{1it}	−0.078[a]	−0.078[a]	0.015
	(0.025)	(0.025)	(0.035)
X_{2t}	0.937[a]	0.937[a]	0.562
	(0.171)	(0.171)	(0.366)
Constant	0.5	0.5	3
	(0.987)	(0.987)	(1.898)
$k = 1$ (low corruption)			
X_{1it}	0.031	0.031	−0.031
	(0.034)	(0.034)	(0.046)
X_{2t}	0.5[a]	0.5[a]	−0.5
	(0.18)	(0.180)	(1.141)
Constant	4.5	4.5[a]	8.0[a]
	(1.223)	(1.22)	(2.63)
Wald chi-square	20.94[a]	20.94[a]	0.46
(*p* value)	(0.000)	(0.000)	(0.794)

Note: Figures in the parenthesis are standard errors.
Corruption perception index (CPI) is available for the period 1995–2010. We have combined CPI series with the previously used income series.
[a]indicates significance at 1% level of significance;
[b]indicates significance at 5% level of significance;
[c]indicates significance at 10% level of significance.

insignificant. The relationship between growth of regional income and growth of national income $(\partial Y_{it}/\partial X_{2t})$ is significant and positive for all time periods and all subgroups.

We also estimate the same model by dividing the 1994–2001 data into two groups based on a regime change. For the case of India, we find a noticeable change in the Corruption Perception Index around the late 1990s. So we have divided the data into two groups around 1999: $k = 0$

for all data points before 1999 and $k = 1$ for all data points on or after 1999. We have presented the results in the third column of Table 5.13. The estimate of coefficient of X_{1it} from the random coefficients model is not statistically significant for either regime (pre- or post-1999). We do see income divergence pre-1999 and income convergence post-1999. The relationship between growth of regional income and growth of national income ($\partial Y_{it}/\partial X_{2t}$) is not statistically significant in either subgroup. In the Indian case, we do not get what one would expect regarding the effect of corruption on income convergence or divergence, because income diverges during low corruption and converges during high corruption. The expected effects are visible only in the context of corruption regime change, but these effects are not statistically significant.

First, we look at the first column of the table of results for China (Table 5.14). Estimate of the coefficient of X_{1it} from the random coefficients model is significant only for the low corruption group for time period 1995–2010. We see income divergence for the high corruption group and income convergence for the low corruption group. The relationship between growth of regional income and growth of national income ($\partial Y_{it}/\partial X_{2t}$) is significant and positive for all subgroups.

We also estimate the same model by dividing the 1985–2010 data into two groups based on a regime change. For the case of China, we find a noticeable change in the Corruption Perception Index around the late 1990s. So we have divided the data into two groups around 1998: $k = 0$ for all data points before 1998 and $k = 1$ for all data points on or after 1998. We have presented the results in the second column of Table 5.14. The estimate of coefficient of X_{1it} from the random coefficients model is statistically significant for the post-1998 regime. We do see income divergence pre-1998 and statistically significant income convergence post-1998. The relationship between growth of regional income and growth of national income ($\partial Y_{it}/\partial X_{2t}$) is positive and statistically significant in both regimes. Corruption has all the expected effects so far as the Chinese experience is concerned.

First, we look at the first column of the table of results for Brazil (Table 5.15). Estimate of the coefficient of X_{1it} from the random coefficients model is significant for the high and low corruption groups for time period 1995–2009. We see income divergence for the high and low

Table 5.14. Regression results for China.

Dependent variable: Y_{it}

	Data sorted by Corruption Perception Index	Data sorted by regime change
	1995–2010	1985–2010
$k = 0$ (high corruption)		
X_{1it}	0.075	0.078
	(0.054)	(0.054)
X_{2t}	0.999[a]	0.973[a]
	(0.029)	(0.024)
Constant	0.180	0.446[a]
	(0.137)	(0.155)
$k = 1$ (low corruption)		
X_{1it}	–0.113[a]	–0.080[b]
	(0.020)	(0.041)
X_{2t}	1.034[a]	1.014[a]
	(0.028)	(0.022)
Constant	0.182	0.161
	(0.137)	(0.143)
Wald chi-square	1251.3[a]	1984.49[a]
(p value)	(0.000)	(0.000)

Note: Figures in the parenthesis are standard errors.
Corruption perception index (CPI) is available for the period: 1995–2010.
We have combined CPI series with the previously used income series.
[a]indicates significance at 1% level of significance;
[b]indicates significance at 5% level of significance;
[c]indicates significance at 10% level of significance.

corruption groups. The relationship between growth of regional income and growth of national income ($\partial Y_{it}/\partial X_{2t}$) is significant and positive for all subgroups.

We also estimate the same model by dividing the 1994–2009 data into two groups based on a regime change. For the case of Brazil, we find a noticeable change in the Corruption Perception Index around early 21st century. So we have divided the data into two groups around 2003: $k = 0$ for all data points before 2003 and $k = 1$ for all data points on or after 2003. We have presented the results in the second column of Table 5.15. The estimate

Table 5.15.   Regression results for Brazil.

Dependent variable: Y_{it}

	Data sorted by Corruption Perception Index	Data sorted by regime change
	1994–2009	1994–2009
$k = 0$ (high corruption)		
X_{1it}	11.375[a]	18.375[a]
	(1.862)	(3.096)
X_{2t}	0.989[a]	0.981[a]
	(0.075)	(0.075)
Constant	0.281	0.244
	(0.358)	(0.354)
$k = 1$ (low corruption)		
X_{1it}	14.5[a]	10.75[a]
	(2.153)	(1.866)
X_{2t}	1.001[a]	0.992[a]
	(0.075)	(0.075)
Constant	0.195	0.257
	(0.360)	(0.354)
Wald chi-square	190.24[a]	189.32[a]
(*p* value)	(0.000)	(0.000)

Note: Figures in the parenthesis are standard errors.
Corruption perception index (CPI) is available for the period: 1995–2010. We have combined CPI series with the previously used income series.
[a] indicates significance at 1% level of significance;
[b] indicates significance at 5% level of significance;
[c] indicates significance at 10% level of significance.

of coefficient of X_{1it} from the random coefficients model is statistically significant for the pre- and post-2003 regime. We also see income divergence pre-2003 post-2003 era. The relationship between growth of regional income and growth of national income ($\partial Y_{it}/\partial X_{2t}$) is positive and statistically significant in both regimes. Table 5.15 shows income divergence and, therefore, an increase in inequality irrespective of corruption.

First, we look at the first and second columns of the table of results for Russia (Table 5.16). Estimate of the coefficient of X_{1it} from the

Table 5.16. Regression results for Russia.

Dependent variable: Y_{it}

	1996–2000	1999–2010	1999–2010
$k = 0$ (high corruption)			
X_{1it}	4	111.734[b]	90.783[a]
	(6.731)	(6.765)	(3.631)
X_{2t}	−3	1.014[a]	1.009[a]
	(2.149)	(0.030)	(0.029)
Constant	288	0.626[a]	0.482[a]
	(246.48)	(0.181)	(0.185)
$k = 1$ (low corruption)			
X_{1it}	0.291	70.96[a]	92.431[a]
	(0.232)	(6.698)	(3.633)
X_{2t}	1.089[a]	1.009[a]	1.01[a]
	(0.182)	(0.030)	(0.029)
Constant	0	0.347[b]	0.463[a]
	(3.24)	(0.180)	(0.186)
Wald chi-square	44.34[a]	1079.89[a]	1872.22[a]
(p value)	(0.00)	(0.00)	(0.00)

Note: Figures in the parenthesis are standard errors.
Corruption perception index (CPI) is available for the period: 1995–2010.
We have combined CPI series with the previously used income series.
[a] indicates significance at 1% level of significance;
[b] indicates significance at 5% level of significance;
[c] indicates significance at 10% level of significance.

random coefficients model is not significant for either the high or low corruption groups for any time period: 1996–2000 or 1999–2010. We see income divergence for the high and low corruption groups. The relationship between growth of regional income and growth of national income $(\partial Y_{it}/\partial X_{2t})$ is significant and positive for most subgroups.

We also estimate the same model by dividing the data into two groups based on a regime change. For the case of Russia, we find a noticeable change in the Corruption Perception Index around 2007. So we have divided the data into two groups around 2007: $k = 0$ for all data points before 2007 and $k = 1$ for all data points on or after 2007. We have presented the results in the third column of Table 5.16. The estimate of coefficient of X_{1it} from the random coefficients model is statistically significant for the pre- and post-2007 regime. We also see income divergence pre- and post-2007 era. The relationship between growth of regional income and growth of national income $(\partial Y_{it}/\partial X_{2t})$ is positive and statistically significant in both regimes. As in the case of Brazil, income divergence in Russia and the consequent growth in inequality cannot be connected with corruption. Corruption seems to have a systematic effect on income distribution only in the case of China. Corruption matters in the other three countries, but not in all circumstances.

5.10. Regression Results with Role of Government Spending

The governmental agencies of any country play a vital role in the overall social, economic, and cultural development of the country. To draw out the importance of the role of government in a country, we estimate the same random coefficient model where the data are sorted according to the size of the public sector or final consumption (C) expenditures by the government.

We maintain the previous definitions of variables, Y_{it}, X_{1it}, and X_{2t}. The dependent variable Y_{it} is the ith region's annual growth rate in year t.[10] To draw out the role of the government in our model, we classify our data according to the size of the public sector or the share of the public sector in total consumption (C/Y), where C is the final consumption expenditure of administrative departments and Y is the net national income. We believe this variable will capture the size of transfers by the government from high income to low income earners. We have sorted the data by the size of transfers and have divided the entire dataset into two subgroups: $k = 1$ for regions where the share of public sector in total consumption is high (i.e., regions of high transfers) and $k = 0$ for regions where the share of public sector in total consumption is low (i.e., regions of low-transfers).

From the random coefficient model, we will be able to estimate a slope coefficient for each independent variable, for every subgroup. Thus, we

---

[10] The region could be a state, province, or Federation Unit; $i = 1, 2, \ldots, N$ and $t = 1, 2, \ldots, T$.

will be able to estimate β_1 or $\partial Y_{it}/\partial X_{1it}$, the relationship between the ith region's annual growth rate in year t (Y_{it}) and the income gap (X_{1it}) for each subgroup, $k = 0$ and $k = 1$. Further, we will be able to estimate β_2 or $\partial Y_{it}/\partial X_{2t}$, the relationship between Y_{it} and the growth rate of aggregate income of the country (X_{2t}) for each subgroup ($k = 0, 1$). The coefficient of X_{1it}, ($\partial Y_{it}/\partial X_{1it}$) will help us determine if income converges or diverges in each subgroup.

For each country India (Table 5.17), China (Tables 5.18 and 5.19), Brazil (Table 5.20), and Russia (Table 5.21), we will look at the relationship between Y_{it} and X_{1it} and the relationship between Y_{it} and X_{2t} for each subgroup ($k = 0, 1$).

5.10.1. Role of the government: India

Figure 5.1 shows how the role of the government has changed in India from 1960 to 2010. We plot the time series of the share of the public sector

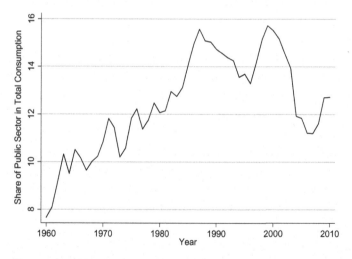

Figure 5.1. Share of public sector in total consumption = (C/Y)*100%; where C = final consumption expenditures of administrative departments and Y = net national income.

Note: Both C and Y are measured in Crore Rupees at current prices.

Source: NAS, Ministry of Statistics and Programme Implementation, Government of India, Back Series 2011 and 2012.

in total consumption $= (C/Y)*100\%$, where $C =$ the final consumption expenditure of administrative departments and $Y =$ the net national income. Both C and Y are measured in Crore Rupees at current prices.

The government consumption includes salaries of government employees and expenditures on purchase of goods and services by administrative departments of the government, that is, state, central, union territory, urban, rural and local authorities engaged in administration, defense, and regulation of public order, health, educational, cultural, recreational and other social and welfare services; promotion of economic growth, and technological development.

The first subgroup ($k = 0$) includes all observations on regions where share of public sector in total consumption is low. For this group, we expect a positive relationship between the ith region's annual growth rate in year t (Y_{it}) and the income gap (X_{1it}). In this subgroup, values of X_{1it} will be positive in some regions (for regions belonging to the affluent group where) and will be negative in some regions (for regions in the deprived group). In the presence of low government transfers, higher the region's income in the affluent group or the deprived group, higher is the gap and faster is the growth rate, thus, leading to income divergence. Note, if the gap is negative, a higher gap for the ith region ($-2 > -3$) indicates that region in more affluent among those in the deprived group. The analysis is reversed for the second subgroup ($k = 1$), which includes all observations on regions where share of public sector in total consumption is high. For this group, we expect a negative relationship between the ith region's annual growth rate in year t (Y_{it}) and the income gap (X_{1it}). In the presence of high government transfers, incomes of the more privileged in the affluent group and the deprived group will grow at a slower rate than the incomes of the less privileged in the affluent group and the deprived group, thus, leading to income convergence.

From the random coefficient model, $\partial Y_{it}/\partial X_{1t}$, the estimated slope coefficient of X_{1it} is positive and significant for the low transfers subgroup ($k = 0$) only during the time period 1999–2008. During this period, we estimate a positive significant relationship between the ith state's annual growth rate in year t (Y_{it}) and the income gap (X_{1it}), implying income divergence. In the same time period, for the high transfers subgroup ($k = 1$), we estimate a negative relationship between Y_{it} and X_{1it}, implying

Table 5.17. Regression results for India.

Dependent variable: Y_{it}

	Data sorted by share of public sector in total consumption		
	1980–1981 to 1996–1997	1993–1994 to 2000–2001	1999–2000 to 2007–2008
$k = 0$ (low transfers)			
X_{1it}	−0.012	0.013	0.051^c
	(0.021)	(0.052)	(0.030)
X_{2t}	0.826^a	0.898^c	1.089^a
	(0.143)	(0.544)	(0.3)
Constant	0.846	0.645	−0.779
	(0.756)	(3.47)	(2.598)
$k=1$ (high transfers)			
X_{1it}	−0.001	0.011	−0.048
	(0.026)	(0.047)	(0.031)
X_{2t}	0.867^a	0.169	0.772^a
	(0.141)	(0.557)	(0.239)
Constant	0.823	5.39^c	1.697
	(0.756)	(2.98)	(1.451)
Wald chi-square	41.26^a	0.9	25.74^a
(p value)	(0.000)	(0.637)	(0.000)

Note: Figures in the parenthesis are standard errors.
All 1980–1997 income data are in 1980–1981 prices, 1993–2005 income data are in 1993–1994 prices, and 1999–2008 income data are in 1999–2000 prices;
^{a} indicates significance at 1% level of significance;
^{b} indicates significance at 5% level of significance;
^{c} indicates significance at 10% level of significance.

income convergence. However, the estimated negative relationship is not statistically significant. The relationship between Y_{it} and X_{1it} is not statistically significant for any other time period.

We see income convergence for states where the share of public sector in total consumption is high (the high transfers subgroup or $k = 1$) and income divergence for states where the share of public sector in total

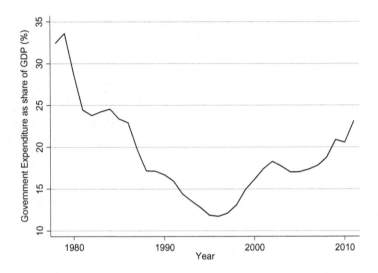

Figure 5.2.   Role of Government in China.

Source: China National Bureau of Statistics, *Statistical Yearbooks* (published annually).

consumption is low (the low transfers subgroup or $k = 0$), only during 1999–2008. The relationship between growth of state income and growth of national income $(\partial Y_{it}/\partial X_{2t})$ is significant and positive for most time periods of all subgroups.

5.10.2.   *Role of government: China*

Figure 5.2 shows how the role of the government has changed in China from 1978 to 2011. We plot the time series of government expenditures as a percent of GDP. Government expenditure includes expenditure on the following main items: government and foreign affairs, defense and public security, education, science and technology, social safety net and employment efforts, healthcare, environmental protection, water conservation, and poverty alleviation. Both government expenditures and GDP are measured in 100 million Yuan at current prices.

The first subgroup $(k = 0)$ includes all observations on regions where the share of government expenditures in GDP is low. For this group, we expect a positive relationship between the ith region's annual growth rate in

Table 5.18. Regression results for China: Two subgroups $k = 0, 1$.

Dependent variable: Y_{it}

	Data sorted by share of government expenditure in GDP		
	1996–2010	1984–2010	1978–1984
$k = 0$ (low transfers)			
X_{1it}	−0.001	0.043	0.091
	(0.058)	(0.041)	(0.075)
X_{2t}	1.027[a]	0.975[a]	1.017[a]
	(0.041)	(0.028)	(0.104)
Constant	0.122	0.304[c]	0.057
	(0.198)	(0.169)	(0.508)
$k=1$ (high transfers)			
X_{1it}	−0.052	−0.041	0.075
	(0.032)	(0.038)	(0.113)
X_{2t}	0.951[a]	0.996[a]	1.141[a]
	(0.066)	(0.030)	(0.055)
Constant	0.622[c]	0.277	0.419
	(0.33)	(0.168)	(0.48)
Wald chi-square	389.16[a]	1799.54[a]	322.03[a]
(*p* value)	(0.000)	(0.000)	(0.00)

Note: Figures in the parenthesis are standard errors.
All 1978–1984 data are in 1978 prices and 1985–2010 data are in 1985 prices;
[a] indicates significance at 1% level of significance;
[b] indicates significance at 5% level of significance;
[c] indicates significance at 10% level of significance.
Source: China National Bureau of Statistics, *Statistical Yearbooks* (published annually).

year t (Y_{it}) and the income gap (X_{1it}) or income divergence. The analysis is reversed for the second subgroup ($k = 1$), which includes all observations on regions where the share of government expenditure in GDP is high. For this group, we expect a negative relationship between the ith region's annual growth rate in year t (Y_{it}) and the income gap (X_{1it}) or income convergence.

We obtain our data from the *Statistical Yearbooks* published annually by the China National Bureau of Statistics. The regional (or provincial data) income data are in constant prices. Regional data on government expenditures are available only in current prices during the time period 1996–2010. Annual data on government expenditures at the national level are available in current prices from 1978 to 2010. To capture the size of the government or level of transfers, we look at the share of government expenditures at the provincial level (or the national level) as a share of total income, that is, the GRP (or GDP) in current prices. For the period 1996–2010, we sort the data by share of regional government expenditures in the GRP. For the periods 1984–2010 and 1978–1984, we sort the data by the share of government expenditures in GDP: $k = 0$ for regions with a small government or low government transfers and $k = 1$ for regions with high government transfers.

From the random coefficient model, $\partial Y_{it}/\partial X_{1t}$, the estimated slope coefficient of X_{1it} is not significant for any subgroup: $k = 0$ or $k = 1$ for any time period. Only during 1984–2010, we observed expected signs. For the low-transfers subgroup ($k = 0$), we estimate a positive relationship between Y_{it} and X_{1it}, implying income divergence. In the same time period, for the high transfers subgroup ($k = 1$), we estimate a negative relationship between Y_{it} and X_{1it}, implying income convergence. However, the estimated relationships are not statistically significant. As expected, the coefficient of X_{2t} is significant and positive for all subgroups and in all time periods.

To investigate further, we also estimate a nonlinear population regression function, where the mathematical component of the function is quadratic. We find the estimates from a nonlinear random coefficient model significant. To capture this result in a linear model, we sort the entire data set by size of government and divide it into four subgroups. The first two subgroups ($k = 0, 1$) include provinces with small government or low government transfers where we expect a positive relationship between Y_{it} and X_{1it}, implying income divergence. The last two subgroups ($k = 2, 3$) include provinces with big government of high government transfers, where we expect a negative relationship between Y_{it} and X_{1it}, implying income convergence. The estimates from a linear random coefficient model, where the data in divided into four subgroups ($k = 1, 2, 3, 4$) are presented below:

In this model with four subgroups, we do find some statistically significant estimates of slope coefficients with expected signs. For example, during

Table 5.19.   Regression results for China: Four subgroups $k = 0, 1, 2, 3$.

Dependent variable: Y_{it}

	Data sorted by share of government expenditure in GDP		
	1996–2010	1984–2010	1978–1984
$k = 0$ (low transfers)			
X_{1it}	−0.003	0.116[b]	0.275[a]
	(0.075)	(0.056)	(0.086)
X_{2t}	1.032[a]	0.964[a]	0.774[a]
	(0.042)	(0.028)	(0.272)
Constant	−0.069	0.518[a]	0.226
	(0.224)	(0.186)	(0.539)
$k = 1$ (low transfers)			
X_{1it}	0.126	−0.059	0.058
	(0.16)	(0.054)	(0.087)
X_{2t}	1.014[a]	1.008[a]	0.917[a]
	(0.044)	(0.029)	(0.272)
Constant	−0.116	0.131	0.587
	(0.238)	(0.186)	(0.745)
$k = 2$ (high transfers)			
X_{1it}	−0.134	0.012	0.153[c]
	(0.151)	(0.055)	(0.086)
X_{2t}	0.979[a]	0.991[a]	1.211[a]
	(0.048)	(0.029)	(0.152)
Constant	0.373	0.289	−0.516
	(0.303)	(0.187)	(0.651)
$k = 3$ (high transfers)			
X_{1it}	−0.041	−0.087[c]	0.009
	(0.049)	(0.050)	(0.098)
X_{2t}	0.934[a]	1.027[a]	1.149[a]
	(0.051)	(0.029)	(0.099)
Constant	0.778[b]	0.052	1.066[c]
	(0.335)	(0.180)	(0.632)

(Continued)

Table 5.19. (*Continued*)

	Data sorted by share of government expenditure in GDP		
	1996–2010	1984–2010	1978–1984
Wald chi-square	433.49ᵃ	1393.84ᵃ	20.37ᵃ
(p value)	(0.000)	(0.000)	(0.000)

Note: Figures in the parenthesis are standard errors.
All 1978–1984 data are in 1978 prices and 1985–2010 data are in 1985 prices;
ᵃ indicates significance at 1% level of significance;
ᵇ indicates significance at 5% level of significance;
ᶜ indicates significance at 10% level of significance.
Source: China National Bureau of Statistics, *Statistical Yearbooks* (published annually).

the time periods 1984–2010 and 1978–1984, we find a positive significant relationship between Y_{it} and X_{1it}, indicating income divergence in the low transfers subgroup: $k = 0$. During 1984–2010, we find a negative significant relationship between Y_{it} and X_{1it}, indicating income convergence in the high transfers subgroup: $k = 3$.

5.10.3. *Role of the government: Brazil*

To find data on the size of government in Brazil, we look at IBGE. Figure 5.3 shows how the role of the government has changed in Brazil from 1995–2009. We plot the time series of the share of the public sector in total consumption $= (C/Y)*100\%$, where $C =$ the final consumption expenditure of administrative departments and $Y =$ the net national income. Both C and Y are measured in Crore Reals at current prices.

The government consumption includes salaries of government employees and expenditures on purchase of goods and services by administrative departments of the government, that is, state, central, union territory, urban, rural, and local authorities engaged in administration, defense, and regulation of public order; health, educational, cultural, recreational, and other social and welfare services; promotion of economic growth, and technological development.

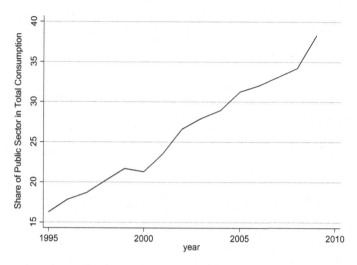

Figure 5.3. Share of public sector in total consumption = (C/Y)*100%; where C = consumption expenditure of public administration in current R$ and Y = purchasing power parity (PPP) converted GDP in current I$.

Source: The source of Public Consumption Expenditures is IBGE and PPP converted GDP data are obtained from the Penn World Tables, Center for International Comparisons of Production, Income and Prices, University of Pennsylvania.

The first subgroup ($k = 0$) includes all observations on regions where the size of government is small and level of transfers is low. We expect to find a positive relationship between the ith region's annual growth rate in year t (Y_{it}) and the income gap (X_{1it}) or income divergence. For the second subgroup ($k = 1$), which includes all observations on regions where share of public sector in total consumption is high, we expect a negative relationship between Y_{it} and X_{1it} or an income convergence. According to the theory, in the presence of high government transfers, incomes of the more privileged in the affluent group and the deprived group will grow at a slower rate than the incomes of the less privileged in the affluent group and the deprived group, thus, leading to income convergence.

During 1995–2009, from the random coefficient model, $\partial Y_{it}/\partial X_{1t}$, the estimated slope coefficient of X_{1it} is positive and significant for the low transfers subgroup ($k = 0$) as well as the high transfers subgroup ($k = 1$). For both subgroups, during this period, we estimate a positive significant

Table 5.20.   Regression results for Brazil.

Dependent variable: Y_{it}

	Data sorted by share of public sector in total consumption 1995–2009
$k = 0$ (low transfers)	
X_{1it}	12.539[a]
	(1.916)
X_{2t}	0.975[a]
	(0.121)
Constant	0.427
	(0.576)
$k = 1$ (high transfers)	
X_{1it}	12.791[a]
	(1.539)
X_{2t}	1.043[a]
	(0.094)
Constant	−0.116
	(0.496)
Wald chi-square	203.84[a]
(*p* value)	(0.000)

Note: Figures in the parenthesis are standard errors.
All 1995–2009 income data are in 1995 prices. The share
of public sector data in national income is in current prices;
[a] indicates significance at 1% level of significance;
[b] indicates significance at 5% level of significance;
[c] indicates significance at 10% level of significance.

relationship between the ith Federation Unit's annual growth rate in year t (Y_{it}) and the income gap (X_{1it}), implying income divergence.

We see income divergence for all regions where the share of public sector in total consumption is high (the high transfers subgroup or $k = 1$) and where the share of public sector in total consumption is low (the low transfers subgroup or $k = 0$). The relationship between growth of state income and growth of national income ($\partial Y_{it}/\partial X_{2t}$) is significant and positive for all subgroups.

5.10.4. *Role of the government: Russia*

We look at the real income data for 79 provinces during the time period 1998–2010 (at 2005 prices) obtained from the Federal State Statistics Service of the Russian Federation (GOSKOMSTAT) and wage data for 88 provinces during 1990–2000 (at 1990 prices) from the Inequality project, University of Texas at Austin.

To find data on the size of government in the Russian Federation, we look at government consumption share of PPP converted GDP per capita at current prices from the Penn World Tables (version 7.1), Center for International Comparisons of Production, Income and Prices (CIC), University of Pennsylvania. Figure 5.4 plots how the role of the government has changed from 1990 to 2009.

The first subgroup ($k = 0$) includes all observations on regions where size of government is small and level of transfers is low. We expect to find a positive relationship between the ith region's annual growth rate

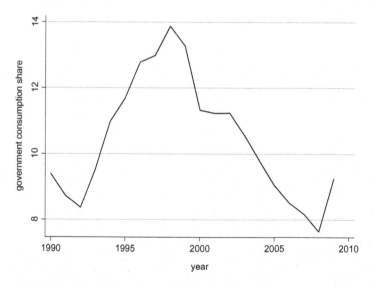

Figure 5.4. The Role of Government in Russia: Government consumption share of PPP converted GDP per capita at current prices.

Source: Heston, A *et al.* (2011), Penn World Table Version 7.0, Center for International Comparisons of Production, Income and Prices at the University of Pennsylvania.

Table 5.21. Regression results for Russia.

Dependent variable: Y_{it}

	Government consumption share of PPP converted GDP per capita at current prices	
	1990–2000	1998–2009
$k = 0$ (low transfers)		
X_{1it}	18.634[b]	72.663[a]
	(9.804)	(2.050)
$(X_{1it})^2$	1.248[c]	102.1[a]
	(0.728)	(41.265)
$(X_{1it})^3$	0.018[c]	87.741
	(0.011)	(321.8)
X_{2t}	0.95[a]	1.005[a]
	(0.035)	(0.043)
Constant	39.263[c]	0.067
	(22.232)	(0.198)
$k = 1$ (high transfers)		
X_{1it}	11.445	87.62[a]
	(9.822)	(5.75)
$(X_{1it})^2$	0.515	113.468[a]
	(0.643)	(24.265)
$(X_{1it})^3$	0.005	300.3[a]
	(0.008)	(128.7)
X_{2t}	0.685	0.993[a]
	(0.485)	(0.055)
Constant	48.963	0.315
	(31.682)	(0.339)
Wald chi-square	46.04[a]	1276.08[a]
(*p* value)	(0.000)	(0.000)

Note: Figures in the parenthesis are standard errors.
All 1990–2000 income data are in 1990 prices and 1998–2010 income data are in 2005 prices. The share of public sector data in national income is in current prices;
[a] indicates significance at 1% level of significance;
[b] indicates significance at 5% level of significance;
[c] indicates significance at 10% level of significance.

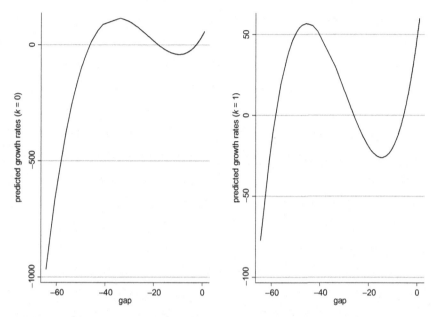

Figure 5.5. Nonlinear relationship between Y_{it} and X_{it} for both subgroups $(k = 0, 1)$.

Data source: Inequality Project, University of Texas, Austin.

in year t (Y_{it}) and the income gap (X_{1it}) or income divergence. For the second subgroup $(k = 1)$, which includes all observations on regions where share of public sector in total consumption is high, we expect a negative relationship between Y_{it} and X_{1it} or an income convergence.

During 1990–2000, the estimated relationship between Y_{it} and X_{1t} from the random coefficient model is a cubic function. We plot the graph of the predicted growth rate versus the income gap for $k = 0$ and 1, in Figure 5.5. The estimated coefficients are significant only for the low transfers subgroup $(k = 0)$ but not for the high transfers subgroup $(k = 1)$. We see income divergence for some regions and income convergence for some regions in both subgroups. The relationship between growth of state income and growth of national income $(\partial Y_{it}/\partial X_{2t})$ is significant and positive for all subgroups.

Again, we use a cubic function to estimate the $Y_{it} - X_{it}$ relationship during 1998–2009. Figure 5.6 provides a graph of the estimated cubic

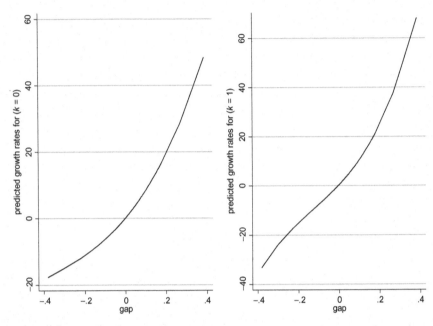

Figure 5.6. Relationship between Y_{it} and X_{it} for both subgroups ($k = 0,1$): A cubic estimation.

relationship between Y_{it} and X_{it} for both subgroups. The slope coefficients estimated from the random coefficient model are significant for both subgroups ($k = 0, 1$). During this period, we find income divergence for regions with low as well as high government transfers. The relationship between growth of state income and growth of national income ($\partial Y_{it}/\partial X_{2t}$) is significant and positive for all subgroups.

Bibliography

Abreu, M (2008), "The Brazilian economy, 1980–1994" in L Bethell (ed.), *The Cambridge History of Latin America*, Vol. 9, Cambridge: Cambridge University Press, pp. 395–430.

Aiyar, S (2001), "Growth theory and convergence across Indian states: A panel study" in T Callen, P Reynolds and C Towe (eds.), *India at the Crossroads: Sustaining Growth and Reducing Poverty*, International Monetary Fund, pp. 143–169.

Arbix, G and MO Salerno (2008), avanço dos países emergentes e o Brasil. *Folha de São Paulo*, São Paulo, Caderno Opinião.

Arnal, E and M Förster (2010), "Growth, employment and inequality in Brazil, China, India and South Africa: An overview" in OECD, *Tracking Inequality in Brazil, China, India and South Africa: The Role of Labour Market and Social Policies*, OECD Publishing, pp. 13–54.

Baer, W (2008), *The Brazilian Economy*, 6th edn. Boulder: Lynne Rienner Publishers.

Banerjee, A and AF Newman (1991), "Risk-bearing and the theory of income distribution," *Review of Economic Studies*, 58, 211–235.

Bardhan, P (1997), "Corruption and development: A review of issues," *Journal of Economic Literature*, 35(3), 1320–1346.

Benjamin, D, L Brandt, J Giles and S Wang (2008), "Income inequality during China's economic transition" in *China's Great Transformation*, Cambridge: Cambridge University Press.

Bhagwati, J and P Desai (1970), *India: Planning for Industrialization*, Oxford: Oxford University Press.

Bhalla, SS (2002), "Growth and poverty in India: Myth and reality" in MG Rao (ed.), *Development, Poverty and Fiscal Policy: Decentralization of Institutions*, Oxford University Press.

Bhalla, SS and P Vashishtha (1988), "Income redistribution in India — A re-examination" in TN Srinivasan and P Bardhan (eds.), *Rural Poverty in South Asia*, New York: Columbia University Press.

Bhatty, IZ (1974), "Inequality and poverty in rural India" in TN Srinivasan and PK Bardhan (eds.), *Poverty and Income Distribution in India*, Calcutta: Statistical Publishing Society.

Biswas, R and A Sindzingre (2006), "Trade openness, poverty and inequality in India: Literature and empirics at the sub-national level," International Conference "The Indian economy in the era of financial globalisation" Fondation Maison des Sciences des l'Homme and Economix, Paris: University Paris, September 28 and 29, 2006.

Borras, SM Jr (2003), "Questioning market-led agrarian reform: Experiences from Brazil, Colombia and South Africa," *Journal of Agrarian Change*, 3(3), July, 367–394.

Brainerd, E (1998), "Winners and losers in Russia," *American Economic Review*, 88(5), 1094–1116.

Brandt, L *et al.* (2008), "China's Great Economic Transformation" in L Brandt and TG Rawski (eds.), *China's Great Transformation*, Cambridge: Cambridge University Press, pp. 1–26.

Cai, F, D Yang and M Wang (2009), "Employment and inequality outcomes in China," Paper presented at the OECD Seminar on "Employment and inequality outcomes: New evidence, links and policy responses in Brazil, China and India," April 2009, Paris: OECD.

Calhoun, C and JN Wasserstrom (2003), "The Cultural Revolution and the Democracy Movement of 1989: Complexity in historical connections" in K Law (ed.), *The Chinese Cultural Revolution Reconsidered: Beyond Purge and Holocaust*, Palgrave Macmillan.

Cartier-Bresson, J (2000), "Economics of Corruption," *OECD Observer*. Available at: oecdobserver.org/news/archivectory.php/aid/239/Economics_of-corruption.html

Danner, J (2006), *Regional Inequality in China: The Role of Public Policy and Investment*, Master's Thesis, The Florida State University, College of Social Sciences.

Das, SK (2005), "Economic foundations of welfare state systems" in B Vivekanandan and N Kurian (eds.), *Welfare States and the Future*, New York: Palgrave Macmillan, pp. 45–51.

Das, SK (2010), "Transparency in government procurement: A case study of India" in A Barua and RM Stern (eds.), *WTO and India: Issues and Negotiating Strategies*, New Delhi: Orient Blackswan, pp. 221-238.

Das, SK and A Barua (1996), "Regional inequalities, economic growth and liberalisation: A study of the Indian economy," *Journal of Development Studies*, 32(3) 363–390.

Das, SK and M Pant (2006), "Incentives for attracting FDI in South Asia: A survey" in *International Studies*, Vol. 43(1) New Delhi: Sage Publication.

Deaton, A (1997), *Analysis of Household Surveys*, Baltimore: Johns Hopkins University Press.

Debroy, B and L Bhandari (2011), *Corruption in India: The DNA and RNA*, New Delhi: Konark Publishers Private Ltd.

Dutt, G and M Ravallion (2002), "Is India's economic growth leaving the poor behind?" *Journal of Economic Perspectives* 16(3), Summer, 89–108.

The Economist (2008), "Economic and financial indicators: Output, prices and jobs," *The Economist*, 387(8586), p. 101, June 28–July 4, 2008.

Fan, S and C Chan-Kang (2005) *Road Development, Economic Growth, and Poverty Reduction in China*, Washington DC: International Food Policy Research Institute.

Flaasbeck, H, S Dullien and M Geiger (2005), "China's spectacular growth since the mid-1990s: Macroeconomic conditions and economic policy challenges" in *China in a Globalizing World*, New York and Geneva: UNCTAD Publication.

Forbes, KJ (2000), "A reassessment of the relationship between inequality and growth," *American Economic Review*, 90(4), 869–887.

Furtado, C (1972), *Formaç ão Econômica do Brazil*, 11th edn. São Paulo: Compantria Editôra Nacional, 45–46.

Galbraith, JK, L Krytynskaia and Q Wang (2004), "The experience of rising inequality in Russia and China during the transition," *The European Journal of Comparative Economics*, 1(1), 87–106.

Galor, O and J Zeira (1993), "Income distribution and macroeconomics," *Review of Economic Studies*, 60, 35–52.

Garbelotti, M (2007), *An Overview of the Strategy of Income Distribution in Brazil*, School of Business and Public Management, The Institute of Brazilian Business and Management Issues — IBI Minerva Program, Washington DC: George Washington University.

Ghosh, J (2010), "Poverty reduction in China and India: Policy implications of recent trends," United Nations Department of Economic and Social Affairs, Working Paper No. 92, ST/ESA/2010/DWP/92.

Griffin, K and Z Renwei (1993), *The Distribution of Income in China*, London: The Macmillan Press Ltd.

Gupta, S, H Davoodi and R Alonso-Terme (1998), "Does corruption affect income inequality and poverty?" International Monetary Fund, Working Paper No. WP/98/76.

Hardt, JP (ed.) (2003), *Russia's Uncertain Economic Future*, Armonk, New York: ME Sharpe.

Hasenclever, L and J Paranhos (2009), "The development of the pharmaceutical industry in Brazil and India: Technological capability and industrial development," Working Paper, Economics Innovation Research Group, Economics Institute, Federal University of Rio de Janeiro.

Herston, A et al. (2008), "China and development economics" in L Brandt and GT Rawski (eds.), *China's Great Transformation*, Cambridge: Cambridge University Press.

Holloway, TH (1975), *The Brazilian Coffee Valorization of 1906: Regional Politics and Regional Dependence*, Madison: State Historical Society of Wisconsin for the Department of History, University of Wisconsin, 5.

Ianchovichina, E, M Ivanic and W Martin (2009), "Implications of the growth of China and India for the other Asian giant: Russia," The World Bank Policy Research Working Paper No. WPS 5075.

International Monetary Fund (2012), *World Economic and Financial Surveys: Regional Economic Outlook*, Table 2.3.

Jain, SD and SD Tendulkar (1990), Role of growth and distribution in the observed change of headcount ratio-measure of poverty, Technical Report No. 9004, Indian Statistical Institute.

Janin, H (1999). *The India–China Opium Trade in the Nineteenth Century*, McFarland, ISBN 100-7864-0715-8.

Jian, T, JD Sachs and AM Warner (1996), "Trends in regional inequality in China," *China Economic Review*, 7(1), 1–21.

Kakwani, N (1986), *Analyzing Redistribution Policies: A Study Using Australian Data*, Cambridge: Cambridge University Press.

Kaldor, N (1956), "Alternative theories of distribution," *Review of Economic Studies*, 23, 83–100.

Kaminski, B (ed.) (1996), *Economic Transition in Russia and the New States of Eurasia*, Armonk, New York: ME Sharpe.

Keane, MP and ES Prasad (2002), "Inequality, Transfer and Growth: New Evidence From Economic Transition in Poland," IZA Discussion Paper No. 448. Available at http://ftp.iza.org/dp448.pdf.

Keidel, A (2009), "Chinese regional inequalities in income and well-being," *Review of Income and Wealth*, 55(S1), 538–561.

Klitgaard, R (1990), *Tropical Gangsters: One Man's Experience with Development and Decadence in Deepest Africa*, USA Basic Books.

Kornai, J (1992), *The Socialist System*, Oxford: Clarendon Press.

Kotwal, A, B Ramaswami and W Wadhwa (2011), "Economic liberalization and Indian economic growth: What's the evidence?" *Journal of Economic Literature*, XLIX(1), 1152–1199.

Kuznets, S (1955), "Economic growth and income inequality," *American Economic Review*, XLV, 1–28.

Lambert, PJ and JR Aronson (1993), "Inequality decomposition analysis and the Gini coefficient revisited," *The Economic Journal*, 103(420), 1221–1227.

Loury, GC (1981), "Intergenerational transfers and the distribution of earnings," *Econometrica*, 49, 843–867.

Lukyanova, AL (2006), "Wage inequality in Russia (1994–2003)," Economics Education and Research Consortium Working Paper Series No. 06/03.

Mani, S (2006), "The incremental innovator vs the trader contrasts between the sectoral system of innovation of the Indian pharmaceutical and telecommunication industries," Globelics India 2006: Innovation Systems for Competitiveness and Shared Prosperity in Developing Countries, Trivandrum, Kerala, October 4–7, 2006.

Martin, LC (2007). *Tea: The Drink that Changed the World*, Rutland, VT: Tuttle Publishing.

Mauro, P (1997), "Why worry about corruption," IMF. Available from: *imf.org*.

Naughton, B (2008), "A political economy of China's economic transition" in L Brandt and T Rawski (eds.), *China's Great Transformation*, Cambridge: Cambridge University Press.

Navarro, Z (1998), "The 'Cédula da Terra' guiding project — comments on the social and political-institutional conditions of its recent development," in *Environment and Planning A* A World Bank document, 37(1–4), p. 259.

Nayyar, G (2008), "Economic growth and regional inequality in India," *Economic and Political Weekly*, XLIII(6), February 09, 2008.

Organisation for Economic Co-operation and Development (OECD) (2007), "Labour markets in Brazil, China, India and Russia and recent labour market developments and prospects in OECD countries" in *OECD Employment Outlook* Chapter 1, Paris: OECD Publishing.

OECD (2010a), *OECD Economic Surveys, China*, Paris: OECD Publishing.

OECD (2010b), *Employment Outlook*, Paris: OECD Publishing.

Ofer, G (1987), "Soviet economic growth: 1928–1985," *Journal of Economic Literature*, 25(4), 1767–1833.

Panagariya, A (2008), *India: The Emerging Giant*, New York: Oxford University Press.

Pant, M (2011), "Indian and the BRICS countries: Issues of Trade and Technology," A study prepared for the center for WTO studies, Indian Institute of Foreign Trade, Ministry of Commerce, Government of India, at the Center for International Trade and Development, School of International Studies, Jawaharlal Nehru University, New Delhi.

Pasinetti, LL (1974), *Growth and Income Distribution: Essays in Economic Theory*, Cambridge University Press.

Persson, T and G Tabellini (1994), "Is inequality harmful for growth?" *American Economic Review*, 84(3), 600–621.

Ravallion, M and G Datt (1990), "Growth and distribution components of changes in poverty measures," LSMS Working Paper No. 83, World Bank.

Rawls, J (1971), *A Theory of Justice*, Cambridge: Mass: Belknap Press.

Rawski, GT *et al.* (2008), "China's industrial development" in L Brandt and TG Rawski (eds.), *China's Great Transformation*, Cambridge: Cambridge University Press.

Rege, V (2001), "Transparency in government procurement: Issues of concern and interest to developing countries," *Journal of World Trade*, 35(4), 489–515.

Remington, TF (2011), *The Politics of Inequality in Russia*, New York: Cambridge University Press.

Remnick, D (1997), "Can Russia change?" *Foreign Affairs*, 76(1), January 1: 35–49. http://www.proquest.com/ (accessed October 28, 2010).

Riskin, C (1987), *China's Political Economy: The Quest for Development Since 1949*, Oxford: Oxford University Press.

Rodrigues, L (2008), Entrevista Jim O'Neill. *O Globo*, Rio de Janeiro, February 03, 2008, *Caderno de Economia*.

Rose-ackerman, S (1999), *Corruption and Government: Causes, Consequences and Reform*, Cambridge University Press.

Rui, H and W Zheng (2009), "Measuring the inter-provincial income inequality in China: A sensitivity analysis," *Journal of Chinese Economic and Business Studies*, 7(1), 55–76.

Sharma S (2007), "China's economic transformation," *Global Dialogue*, 9(1/2), January 1: 29–38, in ABI/INFORM Global [database on the Internet] [cited October 28, 2010]. Available from: http://www.proquest.com/; Document ID: 1929024531.

Song, Z, K Storesletten and F Zilibotti (2011), "Growing like China," *American Economic Review*, 101(1), 196–233.

Swamy, PAVB (1970), "Efficient inference in a random coefficient regression model," *Econometrica*, 38, 311–323.

Tanzi, V (1998), "Corruption around the world: Causes, consequences, scope and cures," IMF Staff Paper.

Tanzi, V and H Davoodi (1997), "Corruption, public investment and growth," IMF Working Paper.

Theil, H (1967), *Economics and Information Theory*, Amsterdam: North Holland.

Thimmaiah, G (2002), "Evolution of tax reforms in India" in MG Rao (ed.), *Development, Poverty and Fiscal Policy: Decentralization of Institutions*, Oxford University Press.

Todaro, MP and SC Smith (2012), *Economic Development*, 11th edn. New York: Addison-Wesley.

Wedeman, A (2012), *Double Paradox: Rapid Growth and Rising Corruption in China*, Ithaca: Cornell University Press.

Wei, SJ (1997), "How taxing is corruption on international investors?" NBER Working Paper No. 6030.

Wei, SJ (1999), "Corruption in economic development: Beneficial grease, minor annoyance, or major obstacle," World Bank Policy Research Working Paper No. 2048.

Williamson, JG (1965), "Regional inequality and the process of national development: A description of the patterns," *Economic Development and Cultural Change*, 13(4) (Pt II).

The World Bank (2001), BRAZIL: An assessment of the Bolsa Escola programs, Report No. 20208-BR.

The World Bank (2004), Inequality and economic development in Brazil, A World Bank Country Study.

The World Bank (2005), Russian Federation: Reducing poverty through growth and social policy reform, Report No. 28923-RU.

Yabuki, S and SM Harner (1999), *China's New Political Economy*, Colorado: Westview Press.

Yueh, L (2010), *The Economy of China*, Northampton: Edward Elgar.

Index